JOURNEY
TO THE
RISE

A candid look at
MOTHERHOOD

Carol M Franklyn PhD

BALBOA.PRESS
A DIVISION OF HAY HOUSE

Balboa Press books may be ordered through booksellers or by contacting:

Balboa Press
A Division of Hay House
1663 Liberty Drive
Bloomington, IN 47403
www.balboapress.com
844-682-1282

Because of the dynamic nature of the Internet, any web addresses or
links contained in this book may have changed since publication and
may no longer be valid. The views expressed in this work are solely those
of the author and do not necessarily reflect the views of the publisher,
and the publisher hereby disclaims any responsibility for them.

The author of this book does not dispense medical advice or prescribe the use
of any technique as a form of treatment for physical, emotional, or medical
problems without the advice of a physician, either directly or indirectly. The
intent of the author is only to offer information of a general nature to help
you in your quest for emotional and spiritual well-being. In the event you use
any of the information in this book for yourself, which is your constitutional
right, the author and the publisher assume no responsibility for your actions.

Any people depicted in stock imagery provided by Getty Images are
models, and such images are being used for illustrative purposes only.
Certain stock imagery © Getty Images.

Interior Image Credit: Benjamin McEachrane

Print information available on the last page.

ISBN: 978-1-9822-6262-4 (sc)
ISBN: 978-1-9822-6263-1 (e)

Balboa Press rev. date: 01/22/2021

DEDICATION

This work is dedicated with love
To my sons
Benjamin and Joshua

ACKNOWLEDGEMENTS

Thank you
to my 'Spirit Posse'
For your unrelenting support
and efforts on my behalf

Thank you
To my sons Benjamin and Joshua
For the lessons in Unconditional LOVE

Thank you
To my husband Fenton
For the Other lessons in Love

Thank you
to my mother Jean and brother Michael
For those early lessons of Love

Contents

||||||||||||||||||||||||||||||||||||||||||||||||||||||||||||||||||||||||||||||||||||||||||||||||||||||||||||||||||||||

FOREWORD   xi

INTRODUCTION   xv

CHAPTER 1
STRESS   1

    Change   5
    Conflict   7
    Frustration   9
    Pressure   11

CHAPTER 2
DISCIPLINE   33

    Delay of gratification   34
    Dedication to reality [truth]   36
    Responsibility   37
    Balance   42

CHAPTER 3
UNCONDITIONAL LOVE   55

CHAPTER 4
THE BIG DECISION   71

CHAPTER 5
SACRED TRUST   87

CHAPTER 6
ADJUSTMENT   95

CHAPTER 7
SPIRITUAL JOURNEY   107

AFTERWORD   127

REFERENCES   141

FOREWORD

It is my hope that the words on these pages will provide helpful information, support and encouragement to mothers as they navigate this life – changing journey. Only few would argue the fact that raising a child is the greatest of responsibilities. Even fewer would argue that well-adjusted children provide considerable hope for our collective future. Why is it then, that mothers-to-be are not encouraged to become more informed about the significant psychological adjustment that is required? Much attention is given to a woman's physical health and fitness both prior to and after the birth – and rightfully so. But equally as important is her emotional fitness to successfully raise a well-adjusted human being. This fitness would be facilitated by knowledge and information, honestly shared, by more experienced mothers who have been through the proverbial trenches. It was my experience however, that there was a paucity of information regarding the "truth of the matter" of motherhood.

A childless friend once shared that several mothers had whispered the words; "If I were you, I wouldn't have any. You're lucky." Then the confession; "I often wish that I didn't do this." It is easier it seems, to admit this to a childless woman although the admission is still whispered. In public, mainly the joys of motherhood are espoused. We are afraid to openly admit to the angst of motherhood. Too bad, for if more of us did, less of us would be so unprepared, less of us would unnecessarily and silently suffer and more time would/ could be spent in the "now" experience with our child. An experience which can be beautiful and awe- inspiring.

So, step number one is for us to be honest with each other. Yes, motherhood can be life's greatest challenge. But it is also one of life's purest joys. It is the closest glimpse of God's face that is daily and readily available. It is also potentially a glimpse of hell! Hence, the conflict. If we openly and honestly admit this to each other as well as to non-parents, we perform a public service. Not only do we release some of our own frustration but we help others to make a more "informed" decision about their parental choice. I do not believe that this kind of honesty would drastically reduce the reproductive activities of the world. I do believe that it would enhance our parental capabilities and therefore the lives of our children, present and future.

Second, we must be aware of the psychological adjustment that is needed. Information regarding what is entailed in such an adjustment could be helpful. The sooner this becomes clear, the sooner one could begin the "practical" aspect of adjustment, i.e. the daily repetition and practice of certain self - statements and other behaviors. We could, before the fact, begin to establish our "village" of supporters. We could be prepared to face personal issues, which are often unearthed by motherhood. Our own fears and our basic assumptions or beliefs about life could be challenged or at least made clear.

In this age of universal spiritual seeking, it behooves us as mothers to foster both within ourselves, as well as within our offspring, that intention towards higher consciousness. Negativity of thought and action do not foster growth, only more suffering and mis-use of time. Negativity of thought poisons us and all whom we influence. It poisons our children. Do not forget that we are indeed spokes of the same wheel. In the case of a mother and child, it often seems as though we are the same spoke on the same wheel. Particularly when very young and dependent, our children look deeply into our faces for messages of love. Do not let them read messages of frustration and resentment. If planning to enter motherhood, some personal work might be in order.

Education in any area, is necessary for development in that area. It also acts to reduce unnecessary anxiety by providing a sense of control and familiarity with the topic. While the old saying "ignorance is bliss" does have some basis in fact (if one prefers to hide one's head in the sand), it is even more true that ignorance is dangerous. Knowledge regarding the processes involved in motherhood should be available to all who plan to embark on this journey. If not for the woman's sake, at least for the sake of the innocent child. We all know that the emotional state of a mother directly impacts her capacity to parent and invariably impacts the emotional health of the child. The idea of pre-baby personal work might seem overwhelming, given all of the other preparatory activities. But it could actually result in less work in the long run – certainly less suffering and more presence in the process.

In this age of information, there is no excuse for being completely ignorant.

KNOWLEDGE IS POWER. BE INFORMED. STRIVE FOR CONSCIOUS ACTION.

INTRODUCTION

They say that "to be forewarned is to be forearmed." Perhaps that is why new mothers are so often taken off guard-so often unaware of the *real* adjustments and changes that accompany motherhood. When veteran moms are dispensing advice and sharing their experiences, they seldom give "the dirt" about this life change. Is it that many forget this initial difficulty as their children grow older and they become more familiar with the requirements of the parenting role? Or is it that they choose to omit this aspect for fear of dissuading new mothers? Perhaps, the fear of appearing "out of control" or less than "Super Mom" is the culprit responsible for this conspiracy of secrecy. Whatever the reason, there are women who feel frustrated, angry and overwhelmed by the whole parenting thing. These are often women who appear on the surface to be very competent, capable and in control. These can even be the professional woman, the woman who has decided to have children a little later in life after having established her career. Some of these women are used to achievement of the highest level. They have towed the line, done the time in terms of academics, work training, degrees. They have proven to the world and to themselves that they are *good enough*. They can bring home the bacon and even fry it up. Then one day they get the news: "YOU'RE PREGNANT."

Whether this is planned or accidental the delivery date arrives. Here is this new mother, beaming with pride [or just because she *thinks* she should be beaming] and a confidence that she can do this – after all, she has accomplished all of those other things in her life. And besides, how complicated could it be to do something so natural, so apparently easy to so many? But as time passes and the fatigue sets in and the expected competence does not quickly or easily appear, she begins to feel out of control. Thoughts such as "Oh my God! What did I do? My life is changed forever! Freedom is a memory!" recur with frightening frequency. Then the doubts about one's maternal instincts emerge. "Maybe I am not the mothering type. Perhaps I am best suited to the office, where things are at least more predictable/within my control and the responsibility is not 24-7." With this new job of parenting there is no time off, no vacation, no escape. So here she is, faced with life's greatest responsibility and convinced that she could not make it through another day or night without rest and some feeling of control. Again, because they are used to being in control, these women do not easily ask for help-especially with such a "natural" task. They suffer quietly, perhaps confiding in friends or the family doctor. They now begin to perpetuate that same conspiracy of secrecy that left them caught off guard. And so it continues.

I am not talking here about postpartum depression or "baby blues." Whether or not a woman has had this experience, there remains an adjustment process to be completed. By this I mean the development of efficient coping strategies which help to achieve the end goal of successful parenting. Even in the generally emotionally stable, the gradual realization that motherhood is much more than anticipated, could test a woman's ability to maintain this stability. So the disillusionment begins. And with it comes anger - often a slow-burning, seething kind of anger which can do insidious damage and result in outbursts of rage as well as emotional distancing from the partner. The fact that the father's life often does not appear to be as rearranged as the mother's is a major fuel to this rage. The expectations of partnership and shared parenting come crashing to the floor as it becomes clear that by virtue of her womanhood, she is expected to take the lion's share of the late nights, changing, feeding and babysitting arrangements. Previously made agreements about 50-50 are not realized for a variety of reasons- the most likely of which is the fact that this is an unrealistic expectation in the first place. That anticipated natural joy of motherhood then seems to be a long time coming.

The one shining light in all of this disillusionment is the love that grows between mother and child. This overwhelming, often first experience with unconditional love, propels the mother forward almost on automatic pilot as she wearily completes the tasks of daily living. This love for the child is almost intoxicating and can make a mother dig deep to find levels of energy that she never dreamed could exist. However, if she continues to do this on a regular basis there will one day be so little energy left that she starts to make statements like "I'm losing my mind, I can't take this anymore." Depression can then follow. Sometimes an obvious, major depression - sometimes a more subtle, low grade, long-lasting sadness.

So what do we do as mothers to avoid getting to this state of fatigue and despair? The state which renders us less than capable of coping with all of our responsibilities, and which [God forbid] reduces our ability to lovingly mother our offspring? How do we make an adaptive adjustment to this new and significant life change?

Of primary importance is an awareness of our basic beliefs, assumptions and expectations about motherhood in particular and life in general. What are we telling ourselves about motherhood? How hard or easy should it be? Exactly what is my end goal here? These questions are asked in several other areas of life. Why not motherhood? Clarity regarding these beliefs is seldom easily or speedily achieved. Many struggle with generating a clear list of their beliefs and habitual self -statements. If we cannot identify these beliefs then we cannot challenge and if necessary alter them. Once we become aware of the fact that like any other life changing event, motherhood places a significant demand on our coping resources, we can consciously work to conserve and replenish those resources. We can endeavor to learn about ourselves and hopefully achieve a higher level of personal as well as spiritual evolution. The term Consciousness comes to mind here. There are several definitions of this word which appear in spiritual and academic writings. But all agree that achieving a higher level of consciousness requires work.

In my opinion and experience, a rise in consciousness means:

- Increased awareness. Awareness of what we think, believe, say and do. Awareness of how these forces influence our daily lives. An intentional, deliberate march towards understanding what drives us.
- Awareness of our divinity, that we are sourced from Love. Realization that Love is the purpose. Awakening.
- A journey from the; "I am alive, I am a person" type of belief, to the highest level of awareness that; "I am light...pure energy... eternally connected to the ALL"
- Approaching the best version of ourselves.

When the well- being of precious charges is involved, we are obligated to do the work – to intentionally embark on a journey towards self-growth and understanding.

It is our spiritual duty to journey to a rise in consciousness.

CHAPTER 1

STRESS

The cry "I am so stressed" is heard in these times all around the world, as a result of many circumstances. But what does it really mean to be stressed? What is a stressor? Put simply, anything that places a demand on a person's system can be described as such. But a demand for what? A demand to cope with or adjust to that stressor. Now the way in which a person copes or reacts to the stressor is not always the most effective. We know that prolonged, unrelenting stress causes fatigue, which compromises all areas of functioning; physical, cognitive/intellectual as well as emotional. Exhaustion and feelings of being overwhelmed are often the result. In motherhood, there is also often a feeling of guilt and even shame upon admitting that these feelings are present. But rest assured, if one mother is having the experience it is likely that many others are as well.

Nowadays, there seems to be a constant sense of urgency. Gotta do this, gotta do that – and NOW.

"Come on kids, hurry up." You just can't wait for them to be in bed, to be asleep so you can wind down, calm down etc. What a waste! A waste of precious time and precious energy. Whether or not we rush through everything, we can still get things done. Maybe they won't get done exactly how or when we want, but eventually. I know - laundry, lunches, housework, homework all have to be done – but maybe with a little less urgency and stress. We miss much that is precious when we rush. We perpetuate a heightened state of physiological arousal when we are always urgent. We feed anxiety and encourage fatigue. We place unnecessary demands on our systems. We feed the erroneous assumption that we can do everything perfectly.

I have adopted the mantra: **URGENCY IS THE ENEMY.** Write that out and stick it on your fridge. Place it in your wallet. Display it in other frequented places around the house. Read it over and over again until it is integrated into the very core of your being. Rehearse it until your behavior automatically reflects it.

LIFE IS NOT A RACE. BE PRESENT. NOW. IN THE MOMENT

ENERGY EFFICIENCY

Any discussion of stress must include the concept of *energy efficiency*. Consider our energy as being held in a cup. If we have a good night's rest, all other things being equal, we should arise in the morning with a full cup of energy. The way in which we use that energy during the day is completely up to each individual. Of course, energy is automatically consumed by the basic bodily functions necessary for life, such as respiration, circulation etc. But we have much more control over how we utilize the remaining energy than we might think. A lot of energy is wasted on unnecessary reactions to circumstances, people and other events. It is important to become aware of the ways in which we waste that energy. We must learn to identify our *energy suckers*. We must learn to pace ourselves. Then we will have much more left for the really important tasks at hand. I suppose this is a version of the old adage to "choose your battles." Remember that the goal is to be as present as possible, with our precious charges.

Sometimes the energy is sucked by our own negativity and inaccurate assumptions or self -statements. Hence the need to identify and dig these out of our consciousness. More often the energy is sucked by our reaction to what others do or do not do. Since we have no control over the actions of anyone but ourselves, let's focus on fixing what we can.

In the interest of successfully managing this precious energy store, it is helpful to understand as much as we can about the sources of our emotional distress. Let's look at some general causes of stress.

Researchers [Weiten and Lloyd, 2000] have described four major types of stress: Change, Conflict, Frustration, and Pressure. Now doesn't this explain a lot! I would assume that the majority of new mothers are experiencing all of these as they try to adjust to their new role.

WHAT WE DO FOR OURSELVES, WE DO FOR OUR CHILDREN

CHANGE

This should be the most obvious of the contributors to stress. You think that you've prepared for the arrival of the baby, and maybe you have. Diapers, baby room etc. *might* all be ready for this change. You might even be somewhat prepared for the sleepless nights and body changes so often talked about by other moms. But what about the *other* changes? What about the intense fatigue and the loss of freedom of movement? What about the loss of the rose-coloured glasses view of the *less than helpful* spouse? What about the realization that YOU are the primary caregiver regardless of pre-baby promises from the partner? What about the anger, sometimes rage? What about the feelings of isolation? What about the slowly emerging sense of incredible responsibility for another human being? What about the feelings of being *trapped?*

What about the fact that you cannot wait to get back to work? Worse yet, what about the realization that you might not *want* to return to work?

With each of these thoughts, can't you just feel the energy being sucked out of your cup?

The greatest change for me was the realization that for the first time in my life, I was experiencing intense, all-consuming, unconditional love. A realization which brought with it a new willingness to be vulnerable. Slowly, I admitted that there was nothing I would not do to protect and take care of this child. Slowly I admitted that there was nothing this child could do to change my love for him/them. I am certain that in this, I am not alone. Talk about a scary change!

**DO NOT ALLOW NEGATIVITY
TO LIVE RENT FREE IN YOUR HEAD**

EMBRACE THE CHANGE

CONFLICT

Conflict can result from opposing wishes, thoughts etc. between two or more individuals. But it also relates to conflict within oneself. I'm sure you can imagine the conflict that could result in a mom's psyche. On the one hand she is overwhelmed and "stressed" by the new demands on her energy source. On the other hand, she is overwhelmed by her love for the child. How does she reconcile these seemingly opposing and often intense states? Acceptance of both, is the answer. Understand that this is part of the process of finding your way through the adjustment. Manage the energy.

A second source of conflict could be the perceived or real lack of help from the partner. This is potentially a major source of argument, resentment and rage. So she goes back and forth in her mind, being happy then being not so happy. She shares the happy with others, [particularly those who expect the happy] and withholds the sad from most. But it takes energy to hold emotions at bay. Result? More fatigue. Again, guard that precious energy.

I know a woman who, in a fit of rage towards her partner and as she stumbled through another load of laundry, desperately cried out to God for strength. All at once, she recounts, the realization dawned on her that; "These are *my* children, *my* responsibility. I will accept any help that I can get from my spouse, but I will not consume my precious energy with resentment." In an instant, she felt relief and a calm not before experienced. Although this state is not easily maintained, with repetition and practice, it can be. Everything takes discipline. So we need to shift our expectations, not to let the partner off the hook, but to conserve energy. More importantly, we do not want to inadvertently transfer that resentment and anger on to the child. Believe me, they are more observant and intuitive than we might realize. They are also innocent. Let's not throw our garbage in other people's yards.

ANGER IS JUST AN EMOTION. IT COMES AND GOES. DO NOT GIVE IT MORE POWER THAN IT DESERVES

FRUSTRATION

What does it mean to be frustrated? We have all experienced this in some form, but seldom stop to define it. Technically, it means that some goal or plan or desire has been blocked or prevented. This failed goal then leads to emotional distress - most likely annoyance, even anger. Certainly, irritability and agitation often result. Some women fear that they might lose control and become "unhinged." But it is preferable to see the frustration as information. It tells you that something needs to be addressed, that those pent-up emotions must be given attention.

It is not necessary to do or say hurtful things in order to express our frustration at this new turn of events in our lives. We should allow ourselves to feel the emotion, acknowledge it, let it wash over you, bawl your eyes out if necessary and then move on.

By the way, it has been my experience that the shower is a wonderful place to let the tears fly. You're all wet anyway and you can emerge feeling emotionally as well as physically cleansed! When we are calmer, we can then try to problem solve and find ways of refilling our energy cups.

We all know that these negative states do not foster best parenting. In the new role of motherhood, there are countless sources of frustration. How are you at frustration tolerance? How long do you stay frustrated when a goal has been thwarted? Do not allow the anger to so build up that it renders you incapable of responsible, loving, child care. While we are seething in the cauldron of *pissed-off-ness*, our innocent children are losing precious time with mom – and we with them. Remember that you've only got *so much* energy to waste. Choose wisely.

EACH TIME WE FALL, RISE, FALL AND RISE AGAIN, WE ARE INCHING EVER MORE CLOSELY TO REAL CHANGE. BE PATIENT. HAVE FAITH. PLANT THE SEED AND THE FRUIT WILL APPEAR

PRESSURE

Oh! This is *the big one* for many of us. Pressure to perform and pressure to conform. Pressure from within ourselves and pressure from external sources.

The first source of pressure is often related to *THE DECISION*. Should I have kids? Do I want to be a mother? Am I expected to do this? And so on. Some feel pressured to reproduce, some feel pressured to decide otherwise. Whatever an individual's decision, there is no need for the often communicated condescension and/or superiority from those in the opposite camp.

It is neither good nor bad to choose motherhood. It is just a choice. When we feel guilty about our choice - whatever that might be - we tend to be over-reactive to the comments of others. We allow ourselves to feel pressure to conform. We become defensive. Whatever your choice, do not be apologetic. Recognize that it was a choice based on your own personal situation. Instead of judging each other's choices, let's be supportive of each other. Respect each other's choice. Mother or not, we can all learn from each other. That we are all in some way flawed, is sufficient evidence of the need for a posture of non-judgement. Ease up on the pressure.

Pressure to perform is both ours to own as well as imposed by others. The expectation of SUPERMOM is the culprit. Again, this takes us back to those old assumptions and beliefs. Do I expect myself to continue to perform at the same level as I did before I was responsible for the care and well-being of another human being? If so, I need to make a quick adjustment here – 'cause that ain't realistic my friend. This is new territory. In spite of past successes in life, we should not expect this to be a *breeze*. A common assumption is that previous competencies [maybe in school or work] would automatically transfer to the job of motherhood. Well, not always. We often have to learn the same lesson in a variety of circumstances in order for the lesson to generalize. So check those expectations at the door and be open to a more easy-going approach. Remember, conserve the energy. Practice, practice, practice.

YOU ARE NOT ALONE.
PAY ATTENTION. HELP IS AVAILABLE

THE BIRTHDAY PARTY EXPERIENCE

I had a meltdown one day - The BIRTHDAY PARTY DAY. Responsibility looming, birthday party arrangements yet to be made. As the day progressed I could feel frustration rising from my gut, gripping my chest, encircling my throat, and eventually resting right between the eyes. I became lightheaded, confused, unable to quickly decision-make as is my habit. I became lacking in focus, unable to prioritize the un- ending list of things to do. Oh my God! What's happening to me? Is this what they call burnout? Will I ever be clear-headed again? I usually go through my errands quite efficiently, listing in order of priority the things that need to be done. But for some reason today, I find myself driving around in circles, uncertain about what to do next. Then a little voice said to me "Just go home, sit and wait." So I listened. I turned the car around and headed for home. I found myself slowly calming down and regaining some clarity of mind.

However as the evening progressed, after having picked up the kids from school and having run around to several places trying to get everything done, I found myself slumped in a corner in the basement, in the middle of a mess to be cleaned up, bawling my eyes out. I was faced head on with the conflict. I adore my children, but I often feel trapped like some animal, pacing around a cage, trying to find a way out. My greatest source of joy and love also at times appears to be the greatest drain on my energy resources.

What kind of a mother am I? What woman would make such a statement? An honest one. I believe that this conflict is secretly a great source of distress for many women. As we know, conflict whether internal or external, is one of the major contributing/determining factors of significant distress. We must not underestimate its impact. Instead be aware of it, face it directly and realize that these overwhelming emotions and fantasies of escape are simply a reaction to the persistent demands placed on our energy. The brain automatically tries to find ways out of situations which are problematic. A number of options might pop into the mind when distressed, but this does not mean that we have suddenly become psychotic mothers, at risk of dangerous behaviour.

We do not really want to "get rid of" our children. But there is a need to get rid of the feelings of desperation and reclaim even a little of ourselves. There can develop within us such a heightened state of arousal that our nervous system is always "on." We are over-stimulated both by external as well as internal stimuli. It is essential to become aware of the various sources of stimulation and learn to regulate them. We must become more efficient in the consumption of our precious, limited energy.

As the day progresses and we go about our various activities and responsibilities, the level of energy in our cup slowly decreases. Some of the energy that is consumed is necessary. Surprisingly, much of the energy that we use is wasted-unnecessarily consumed. Our challenge is to learn to identify and then eliminate those ENERGY SUCKERS in our lives.

These could be activities, various media, certain foods and even people. Pay attention to the way that you feel in response to any of these things. How does a particular television show affect you? Is the level of excitement, danger, violence or even news information in a TV or radio program worth the increased nervous system arousal that almost invariably results? Following the experience, does your cup feel replenished or depleted? After an interaction with that particular individual [friend, coworker, family member] do you feel drained or refueled? Make it a habit to ask yourself this question in relation to any activity in which you engage. You will be shocked to realize how much energy you waste on a daily basis, leaving less available for the important duties of motherhood. Of course, there are certain unavoidable interactions and activities which are by nature energy sucking. However, we can definitely learn to so jealously guard our personal environment that the unnecessary use of energy is brought to a minimum.

Remember, the goal is to be present, in the moment with your children.

IF YOUR CUP IS EMPTY
SO IS YOUR PRESENCE!

SLOW DOWN!

Have you ever felt more stressed when people admonish "slow down?" While it is true that being too fast paced is potentially dangerous, it also seems that the instruction to slow down is yet another "to do" item to be added to the already lengthy list. How am I supposed to slow down when my children need me to provide, spend time and take care of them? How can I slow down if bills are to be paid, meals are to be prepared, laundry is waiting to be done and other household chores are looming? What about ensuring their present comfort and future educational expenses? How can I slow down if I want to work at my career? Choices, choices, choices.

One approach is to stop seeing our responsibilities as weights, and switch the perspective to seeing them as fantastic opportunities. Instead of using words such as "too busy" use words such as "active, occupied" etc. If we have chosen to have a nice house, trips, an education fund, we have to work for it. No, I am not running a campaign for workaholism. I am merely pointing out that with a change in how we view and label our life circumstances, can come a change in perceived stress. What we tell ourselves is what we feel and how we will likely behave. It is now common knowledge that thoughts are creative - whether of tonic for the body or of poison. We can learn to better control the flow of these thoughts, towards the goal of functional efficiency. By this, I mean that we can learn to function more like an economy car than a gas guzzler. It should not take an entire tank of gas to travel a distance that could be covered with a quarter of a tank.

If you learn to identify those "energy suckers" in your life, and then work to systematically eliminate as many of these as possible, you can have more left for important issues such as your children. This identification process could result in some personal closet cleaning. It is not only thoughts, but also certain behaviours, and even people, which result in a loss of energy. It could be necessary to reduce time spent in certain activities, such as watching depressing television programs or listening to music with negative lyrics. It could mean reducing the amount of time spent with negative individuals who leave you emotionally exhausted and more depressed after their visit. Yes, these could (and often do) include well- meaning friends and family.

<u>SUMMARY</u>

Fatigue is a highly underestimated enemy of the human psyche. It robs us of the ability to effectively process or make sense of information. We become unable to deal with many sources of information at the same time. Multi-tasking becomes challenging. Fatigue weakens our resolve to be emotionally constant, to be patient with our offspring as well as partners. We cannot give them our best. When we are fatigued, gloom descends with a frightening intensity. We become less positive, less resourceful and less tolerant. We become less secure and more fearful when we are tired. Why do you think that things always look better in the light of day, after a good night's sleep? It is because a rested mind makes for a more competent, effective and efficient individual. The advice to "get rest" is not to be ignored. It could make the difference between success and failure as a parent.

So, we can see that energy efficiency is Boss! Our energy is also finite. The advice to "take a break" is not just some trite dictum handed down by relaxation gurus. If you know that the gas tank of energy is almost empty and you do not refuel – You WILL stall. If we look at the early experience of motherhood, we can see that there is change, conflict, frustration and pressure involved. But there is also BIG LOVE.

At least partially due to the secrecy of other suffering mothers, you could feel as though you are *the only one*. Your personal experience becomes very intense. You feel guilt and shame and alienation from others – because nobody else seems to be going through or has gone through the same thing. Most others seem happy, content. But you seem weak, ungrateful, A BAD MOTHER.! Enter a few hormonal changes, ups and downs, sleep deprivation and an instant loss of freedom and you end up with a response of emotional distress – periodically intense and potentially dangerous to both mother and child. This is not a thing to be taken lightly, to be dismissed as *female nonsense*. Infants and their mothers, their families are being hurt emotionally and sometimes physically as a result of the mother's distress and lack of support. It must be reinforced in the minds of women that their experience is not unique and that the adjustment can be emotionally overwhelming. It must not be taken lightly the sense of burden and inescapability felt by many. The treadmill of responsibility and duty seems never-ending and exhausting.

In certain cases the result is less than optimal parenting. In some cases it is downright poor parenting. In too many cases it is abuse; mental, emotional and yes, even physical abuse.

Taken lightly, the suffering of an overwhelmed mother can and has ended in tragedy. It is time to hear the silent cries of overburdened moms. It is time to admit and to acknowledge the fact that in spite of competencies in other areas, many women struggle daily, intensely and in silence, with the pressures of motherhood. We have become so accustomed to and even expectant of ease/convenience that any slight deviation from *easy* can generate distress.

It is time for us to admit that in spite of overwhelming feelings of love for our offspring, there are days when we might regret the decision to take on the responsibility. This admission is only heard by close friends and therapists. This admission is also denied by other apparent *supermoms*. But there is good news – You're not alone.

ANY DEMAND ON OUR EMOTIONAL
RESOURCES IS BEST MET WITH CALM

BE AWARE OF YOUR INFLUENCE
ON THE LITTLE ONES
YOUR WORDS AND ACTIONS
CAN HEAL OR HARM

PAUSE, REFLECT

THEN ACT

<u>THINGS TO REMEMBER</u>

Know that you are not alone. Your feelings, thoughts and fears are not uncommon. No One is *that* unique that our experience could not be of benefit to *someone*.

Surround yourself with the positive statements, mantras, beliefs that you would like to integrate into your psyche and replace the negative ones. Write these out and put them on the fridge, in the bathroom, the car, in your wallet – wherever your eyes frequently rest. This way you will have ready access to uplifting statements which could quickly redirect your attention and counteract negativity.

Emotions persist if they are fed by thought. Negative thoughts produce negative emotions. Positive thoughts produce positive emotions. In a word, what we feed grows. So when those negative self - statements emerge, quickly push them back and replace with a more positive one. Gratitude statements work really well here. When in the throes of distress, it might be very difficult to generate those positive thoughts – hence the importance of already having them strategically placed in our familiar environment.

Do not pay attention to every little annoying thing. Choose wisely where you place your attention. That is where you will also spend your energy. Simplify, in the interest of efficiency.

Do not interpret everything that your spouse/partner does/does not do as a personal insult or as negligence of the child. Remember that individuals are in many ways different. Focus on doing YOUR best.

Remember that a lot of your perceived stress could be self-imposed. You do not HAVE to feel the way that you do. It is at least partially due to your own expectations and beliefs about life in general and motherhood in particular. Be kind to yourself.

Do not allow yourself to continually wallow in emotionality. It negatively impacts attention, concentration and sometimes even memory functioning. It hinders the ability to effectively problem solve, make good judgements and decisions. It also distracts you from the task at hand. So relax and focus. Better focus, better results.

While it is true that performance is often enhanced by a certain level of alertness or physiological arousal, it is also true that we can experience diminishing returns from *too much* physiological arousal. More is not always better.

Learn to identify personal indicators or clues that you might be approaching stress overload. Stop yourself before it's too late. Talk to yourself out loud if necessary. PACE yourself.

Remember that you are in "energy conservation mode" here. Do not waste your precious fuel on useless trips to self-pity town and rumination city. If you do, the car will run out of gas. The cup will empty prematurely.

Whenever possible, make self-nurturing a scheduled event. Watch comedy shows and movies that uplift. Plan times of retreat so that you have something to which you can look forward.

Be aware of your limits.

Ask for help.

Seek professional help if unable to regulate your emotions, negative thoughts or behaviours.

Do not make the child collateral damage.

A NOTE TO VETERAN MOMS

PERHAPS PERHAPS PERHAPS

Perhaps   Women today are "soft" compared to those in the *old* days

Perhaps   Women today are too hard and insensitive, too concerned with issues of "I" and not willing to self-sacrifice as women of old used to do

Perhaps   Women today have more choices, making their role confusing and conflicted

Perhaps   Women today are just too busy

Perhaps   That women's rights movement has freed us to choose

When I'm in crisis- who cares? Just give me some acknowledgement, some encouragement, some reassurance and **PERHAPS** some helpful hints.

Veteran moms, just tell me the truth - that you too have had dark days of doubt and conflict. Tell me that you can empathize with my feelings of loss and desperation. Tell me that it will not always be this way. Tell me that I am not alone. Let me share in the fruits of *your* labour. Teach me what you have learned. Do not leave me faltering, repeating lessons already learned, making mistakes already corrected by other members of the *mommy* club.

Do not watch with calm detachment as I struggle to adjust to this new role in my life.
Help me. Help each other.

A SECOND NOTE TO VETERAN MOMS

I WISH

I wish, when in my deepest despair
and greatest overwhelmed-ness
That someone had said to me
"This is your spiritual choice
A grand opportunity
Unconditional love's stage"

I wish someone had said
"Snap out of it! Perspective!
See this as you should!
Practice discipline. Stop whining."

I wish that other women would stop saying
"And it only gets worse"
In reference to teenager-hood

I wish I had the courage to shout
"Why don't you encourage me fellow moms?
Why don't you affirm my strength?
Why don't you reassure and remind me of
the divine blessing that is my new role?
Why don't you show me discipline?
Why don't you welcome me in the *club*
and sincerely share your own feelings?

Why don't you help me?"

A PERSONAL NOTE ON DENIAL

We've all heard the statement "You're just in denial." We can probably think of several instances in which we indeed chose to deny the obvious. We do this in at attempt at avoiding certain truths about ourselves – truths that are incongruent with our Ego's view of ourselves. In short, we need to see ourselves as more virtuous and capable than might actually be the case. The following is a humorous example of the folly of denial.

I was sitting in the dining room of a popular pizza joint in town, having lunch with my two sons, Benjamin age 6 and Joshua 4. This was how the conversation went:

Mom: So, we have to decide what we're going to do about summer.

Benjamin: I want to stay at home with you.

Joshua: I want to go to St. Clair [summer program].

Benjamin: But Joshua, if we go to St. Clair we won't be together. We won't be in the same class.

Joshua: I'm OK with that. I'll be OK.

Mom: Well, I'll tell you what we'll do [attempting to compromise]. We'll go to St. Clair 2-3 days a week and stay at home the other 4 days. That way Benjamin gets what he wants, Joshua gets what he wants and I get what I want.

Benjamin: Freedom! That's what YOU get.

Mom: [I am stunned. All at once, feelings of guilt, awe and a little fear race through my being. I finally mutter sheepishly] How do you know that? Did someone tell you that? To which he responded…

Benjamin: No. I just know. It just came to me.

Mom: [Now I'm *really* guilty. I think Oh my God! My children know that I want time away – to myself- they know that I am not Superwoman – They KNOW!! My mouth finally works again, having dropped almost to the floor and I stutter] Well, what do you mean? What does freedom mean? [If I thought that I was stunned and guilty before, this next response really floored me]. My 6 year-old son said….

Benjamin: No clients. No kids. Just a free woman at home, doing whatever she wants.

I did not realize until that moment that my feelings were so transparent or that my guilt was so deep. I found myself saying "Well, is that OK with you?" Can you believe it? Here I was, asking my 6 and almost 5- year-old sons for *permission* to take care of myself. What the heck was my problem? No wonder I felt like a lump of stress. I was so tightly wound, so guilty, so invested in "doing the right thing always" that I was internalizing the *superwoman* myth. Happily, he replied:

Benjamin: Sure Mom. It's OK.

So...you think it's a secret? Think the kids don't know? Ha! You're the one in denial. The good news is that we can take ourselves off the guilt hook by realizing that wanting free time is not only common, but healthy. After all, "If Mom's not happy, nobody's happy."

You want a happy household? Take care of yourself. You'll be much better able to take care of your family.

CHAPTER 2

||||||||||||||||||||||||||||||||||||||||||||||||||||||||||||||||||||||||||||||||||||||||||||||||||||||||||||||||||||||||||||

DISCIPLINE

A favourite author, Dr. M. Scott Peck [1978] defines discipline as "the basic set of tools we require to solve life's problems." He identified four tools that constitute discipline: delay of gratification, dedication to the truth, acceptance of responsibility and balance. That discipline is a *magic bullet* could be a daunting thought to a woman in the throes of frustration. Daunting because there seems to be little energy left for self-control and doing what needs to be done.

One of the problems here is that the word *discipline* conjures up visions of military bases and army uniforms, of men and women pushing themselves to physical extremes in preparation for battle. But these tools of discipline could help a mother to gain clarity as to the mechanism by which she could gain better control of her emotions and behavior. In my experience as both a mental health professional as well as a mother, there is an inherent frustration which results when individuals are given vague, abstract coping advice. Some pretend to understand the advice and nod blankly in agreement. Some more courageous women cry "What does that mean? How do I become more disciplined? Tell me exactly what to do!"

DELAY OF GRATIFICATION

Have you ever noticed just how self-absorbed humans can be? Yes, ALL of us. Have you noticed that when we become singularly focused on our own needs and their lack of fulfillment, how much internal turmoil follows? Why do we not learn that to be so concerned about how we feel is to cultivate unnecessary suffering? We **MUST** learn to delay personal gratification. Indeed, we must learn that the gratification of those seemingly urgent personal needs is not necessarily what is best for us – both in terms of practical issues as well as personal growth. Let's ask ourselves "What do I want to accomplish here? Am I as dedicated as I think to the best interest of my children? Do I *really* want to be an example of love in both word and deed?" If so, the delay of gratification is in order.

It is certainly a means towards the end of cultivating and modeling discipline. Once the child is able to understand, do not hesitate to inform them of your goals. Let them witness the self-talk that enhances right action.

PUT THEM FIRST – There is a time to happily place the needs of your children above your own. There is a time to embrace the concept of sacrifice. In this era of Individuality and ME-ness we must strive to lovingly and happily accept the primacy of the child's needs. This is not to suggest that we neglect ourselves. I am suggesting that we remember "A season for everything." It *is* possible to accomplish all that we want in life – Just not all at the same time. Sometimes to do the right thing we have to be steady and give up the thing that the ego wants the most – in the moment. Do not risk long term growth for short term relief. Let your behavior be a choice – not a reaction. Do your best with your child. Your time will come.

A child's experience of being primary in importance, of having their needs met and their preferences considered will enhance their esteem and sense of worth. This can work in the future to insulate them against the onslaught of life's challenges. The memory of a caring mother can provide the emotional resource to reach high and dig deep – because you know your value – you've been unconditionally loved. You've been someone's priority.

DEDICATION TO REALITY [TRUTH]

Dedication to the truth, to the reality of the matter requires courage. It is a dedication to honesty regarding the challenge of this new situation. It is a dedication to honesty about our shortcomings and fears. It requires willingness to be flexible about our beliefs and ideas regarding motherhood. It does not serve us to deny or lie about our feelings. A problem denied is a problem left unsolved. Plus, it is far too energy - sucking to maintain a defensive posture regarding our weaknesses and distress. Do not be afraid to learn some truths about yourself. So what if you're not perfect at this? There **is** no perfect at "this."

Yes, facing truth can be painful. But there is pain with gain and pain without gain. You choose. What are you willing to learn? Are you ready to see that you can be selfish, self-absorbed and emotionally reactive? Are you also willing to learn that you can be open, strong, resilient and right-acting? Whatever your truth, it is a stepping stone. You choose where the stones lead.

RESPONSIBILITY

Acceptance of responsibility for our children is supposedly a "no brainer" – Right? I disagree. I believe that it should be a conscious choice, a deliberate and informed intellectual commitment to their well- being. The buck stops here, so to speak. The realization that a partner might not share equally in the responsibility of raising a child has the potential to generate resentment and ultimately waste precious energy. Once you have concluded that this is "My" responsibility, you can move on with less resentment, to fulfill the tasks of the job. Any assistance from the partner is of course welcomed, but might be considered "gravy." Acceptance of responsibility allows us the opportunity to gain wisdom and to practice love. If we do our best in spite of anyone else's behavior, we also provide a good model for the child.

When the emotional resources are running low, the resolution to be responsible can take over and run the show. When a child's needs are involved, "I don't feel like it" just doesn't cut it. We must try our best and better than our best to be reliable and worthy of their trust. Let's strive for consistency and predictability in our actions. Of course we won't always succeed but we have to try. Teach by example.

While it is important to get as much rest as possible, it is equally so to learn to push through fatigue, to perform in a disciplined, consistent manner those duties that we have accepted. The feeling of accomplishment and the experience of untold inner strength is incomparable. It is often in times of extreme frustration, fatigue and even despair that we learn our potential. It is amazing what we can do if pushed, when alternatives are absent.

It is astonishing what we can do when we consciously choose to encourage thoughts and behaviours that are the forerunners of *gut-level competence.*

Point your intentions in the direction of strength – true strength. The strength that comes from deep within - that comes from the conviction that in spite of what our undisciplined bodies are telling us, our disciplined minds will rise to the occasion and do what is necessary.

Learn to detach from the labels "overwhelmed" and "overworked." You will be astounded by how much more energy is potentially available. Do not underestimate the power of determination.

Discipline and commitment go hand in hand. If we do not practice and remind ourselves daily of our goals, we do not progress as well. At the very least we stand still. At the worst, we regress.

TAKE RESPONSIBILITY

IT IS FREEING, LIFE CHANGING, ENERGY CONSERVING

ALWAYS STRIVE FOR JOY AND LAUGHTER THEY ARE WONDERFUL MEDICINE

"BUT IT'S *SO* HARD"

Ease is not a prerequisite of effort

So what if it's hard?
Try anyway

Keep trying and trying
Until the effort becomes
Automatic

Keep trying until
The right response becomes
Automatic

Keep trying until
Right-acting is easy

Keep trying until
Ease becomes the result
Of effort

THERE IS ALWAYS A CHOICE IN LIFE

WE MIGHT NOT LIKE ALL OF
THE CHOICES BUT THERE
THEY ARE NONETHELESS

YOU CAN CHOOSE YOUR
REACTION - ALWAYS

<u>ON RESPONSIBILITY</u>

I resolve to happily, gratefully,
graciously and most of all lovingly
Accept the blessed responsibility
That is
Motherhood

No longer the expectation of 50-50
No longer the need to have 50-50
No longer the feeling of Victimization
Ever after the realization of my great fortune

To be mother
To *feel* mother
To delight in motherhood
That of all, is my quest
That of all, is my gift

BALANCE

Balance is an essential component of stress management. If we do not avail ourselves of rest we will surely reach a point of exhaustion. We have all been bombarded in the past years with the terms "balance" and "time management." And rightfully so. These are keys to a successful adjustment to change in one's life. In fact, "a time for everything" should become a mantra. In particular the setting of priorities would help us to automatically choose the "right" activities in which to spend our precious time. As much as we would like to believe that we could squeeze out more hours in a day, we cannot. Twenty-four hours is all you get in one day, so we just have to make the best of it.

"Take care of yourself." This might sound trite, over-stated, but it is profound. What we do for ourselves, we do for our children. When we have more energy and personal satisfaction they too feel energized, good about themselves and their place in our lives – in our hearts. That little treat, the manicure, pedicure or trinket reminds us of our other identity. It reminds us that we are still undomesticated human beings. We perhaps get a glimpse of the time when pampering ourselves and enjoying freedom was the norm. But in all things – moderation is key.

There are rules of right-functioning which if consistently applied, result in balance. To be specific, accept and expect that there will be easy, challenging, tiring, wonderful, un-nerving, frightening, hopeful, happy and sad times in child-rearing. Live daily in the mind that is aware of the range of possibilities and ready to meet each one as it comes. Do not wait for a situation to arise before planning a coping strategy. Nurture an attitude of strength and competence. Visualize yourself getting through whatever might come your way. Visualize yourself "capable."

You do not necessarily have to "feel" capable – but you can think and act it anyway. "Fake it 'till you make it" and you will eventually get to the place where you feel it. Start NOW.

<u>SUMMARY</u>

O.K. So you're up a creek! Well, here's a paddle. There IS a magic bullet – DISCIPLINE. When we learn to accept the fact that work/effort is required in most things in life we are less prone to wallow in self-pity and we open the door to a more pro-active approach to our difficulties. Ask yourself what can be altered in order to effect positive change. Of course, it is sensible to discriminate between useless and useful effort. For example, we can spend our time working on "worry" but we all know of its ineffectiveness. We could also go the other way and use too much energy in attempts at significant change. Let's use the old trick of balance. Let's remember to be efficient. As little effort for as much gain.

Self-discipline is a cornerstone of growth. We can train our minds to control or at least limit the occurrence of those maladaptive thoughts that take us down a path of emotional demise and result in bad behaviour. As is the case with all skills to be developed, practice is essential. Motherhood is no exception.

It almost appears that discipline is a bad word in many circles. The idea that becoming a good

mother requires much repetition and practice is often met with condescension by those who view this task as "natural and wonderful." "You shouldn't have to work at it!" they scoff. Well, good for them. Many of us *do* require the practice. Deliberate, conscious intent towards improving our performance on the mother-front is essential and facilitative of adjustment. It is certainly beneficial to our charges.

Eventually, as time passes and with more conscious practice, you will no longer find yourself saying "one more day under my belt – I've held it together for one more day." Instead, you will find the days passing more effortlessly. The dread and anticipatory anxiety of another day "in the mom trenches" will surely subside. But remember to see each "mistake", each regretted behaviour as an instructional tool in our motherhood education. With practice, repetition and sometimes immediate feedback regarding our wrongness or rightness, we learn to make less boo-boos and to hurdle many of the pitfalls. Hopefully, we learn to relax and enjoy the journey.

As I watched the movie "Mulan" with my children I was struck by the words in her song "*When* will my reflection show who I am inside?" At that moment I resolved that NOW! NOW, will my reflection show who I am inside. These words have been written on the desk pad in my office in full view as an ever – present reminder of the goal. The goal towards a better, more evolved *me*.

If nothing else, the children deserve that I try.

ANOTHER MAGIC BULLET- GRATITUDE

It is my strong belief that gratitude is magical. Deep, sincere gratitude for even the smallest of things can generate a calm and perspective bar none. Engaging in the exercise of gratitude can provide a positive distraction from negativity and refocus the mind towards effective coping.

One night, as I struggled with my last ounce of energy, thinking that my life was so stressful and filled with responsibility, I decided to channel surf before going to bed. My eyes locked onto a program on the channel guide featuring mothers. So I selected that channel and sat back. There, standing with courage and with pain, were women who had lost their children to violence in the streets of America. As they each spoke to the audience with eloquence and with passion, I felt their pain rise up in my chest. Their dead children were suddenly *my* dead children. And I sobbed. No! I wailed – at the thought that they would never have the opportunity to again say "Oh my God! These children are stressing me out. Motherhood is too hard."

I bet that those women would trade places with me in a second. Suddenly, I was less tired and deeply grateful for my *normal* days of activity and yes – of hope. Suddenly, compared to their loss, child-rearing fatigue became a privilege. **PERSPECTIVE.** I ran upstairs and kissed my sleeping sons. It is amazing the strange and wonderful ways in which the universe provides us with encouragement when we need and ask for it. Nurture an attitude of gratitude – Always and in *all* ways.

Motherhood is like many other jobs in that it takes time to get good at it. Many do not automatically become organized, effective and efficient by virtue of their sex. We learn at different paces and we adjust at different speeds. It is not a competition. It is not about speed. It is about ENDURANCE and LOVE.

I recall reading somewhere that we should appreciate the "normal" days. This is very difficult for many new mothers to accept, as they daily struggle to make the adjustment to their new responsibilities. But there is much truth and wisdom in that statement.

As a person whose daily work involves coming face to face with individuals who in some way are also struggling with adjustment to significant changes, I have learned that a "normal" day is a blessing and to be cherished. A day when all of our body parts work, when our senses are intact, when we can function independently, when we are pain free is indeed a blessing and not to be taken for granted. A "normal" day is one where we know what we have to do and we do it. In spite of fatigue, boredom or frustration we have that commonality of predictability. Predictability can be a blessing. Celebrate sameness, status quo. Be glad that you do not have to be vigilant, awaiting the next tragedy, as is the case with so many of the people that I have served.

I am not suggesting that gratitude must always be comparative. We do not have to look very far to see others who might be better or worse off than we are. We can experience intense gratitude for something as basic as the Life Force that flows through us – through all of us.

When the temptation to complain about the mundane arises, stop yourself. Give thanks for predictability and honour each moment. We are always admonished by spiritual leaders to fully experience "the moment", to mindfully attend to each task great or small. This is not some arcane piece of advice meant to confuse us. This has practical value. It keeps us focused on the task at hand and prevents our tendency towards self-indulgent dissatisfaction. It controls information overload. It helps us to effectively pace ourselves and conserve energy.

Like discipline, gratitude helps us to show up every day – to reflect who we *aspire* to be inside.

YOU ARE CAPABLE OF MUCH MORE THAN YOU REALIZE

DIG DEEP

YOU WILL FIND GOLD

<u>REMEMBER</u>

There are times when we can forge ahead, soldier on. There are times when like the good military strategist we should retreat, regroup, refuel and come out fighting again. Reflect your strength, not your fear.

Do not expect 50/50 from your partner. That is a recipe for disappointment and resentment. Do not expect the partner to "understand" how you feel or to know what to do to make you feel better. They are not you. Be clear about what you want done. Instead of saying "Why don't you help me more?" Say "Could you bring me a diaper, or warm the bottle, or take the clothes out of the dryer?" Be as specific as possible. Do not waste time and/or energy being upset that your partner cannot anticipate your needs.

You cannot throw off the responsibility. Try to learn, within your capabilities, to cope with it, to embrace and appreciate and love the experience.

Remember that the child is a blessed responsibility. Fair or not, it is at times more adaptive, more energy conserving to just do what you have to do for your children without focusing on what the other partner is *not* doing. There is a time to discuss these imbalances in child care, but you must choose time and place wisely.

Do not externalize blame for your feelings. Avoid feelings of entitlement to this or that.

Make flexibility one of your mottos. It's OK to arrange child care.

Reassess your expectations. Make adjustments as necessary. Resolve to roll with the punches so to speak. Be silly. Dance and sing around the house. The children will love it.

Do not wait for the children to be asleep before you see them as 'Angelic.'

Do not waste your time living in the future. Be present and enjoy the nest full.

PRACTICE PRACTICE PRACTICE

CHAPTER 3

||||||||||||||||||||||||||||||||||||||||||||||||||||||||||||||||||||||||||||||||||||||||||||||||||||||||||

UNCONDITIONAL LOVE

The question "Why do you love me?" has been posed in numerous media by countless individuals. I have always balked at the list of attributes and reasons offered in response to this question. "I love you" because you are this or that, because you make me feel this or that, seems a description of a *conditional* love. Absent these stated reasons and the love disappears? Shouldn't love be unconditional? Isn't *real* love unconditional?

Motherhood has been my crash course in unconditional love. Admittedly, it made me challenge my previously held assumption that I knew what it was to love without condition. Upon reflection, it became clear that this was some *different* kind of love. This was not a love *because of* anything. It was a love *in spite of* everything. In spite of the fatigue, loss of freedom, responsibility and fear associated with this new role, *this* love was big and all-consuming and delicious and energizing and inescapable.

This was the "I will love you no matter what" kind of love. Terrifying! Talk about the realization of vulnerability, of the willingness to *be* vulnerable – for the first time. So this is what mothers have been talking about. This is what fuels a mother's ability to lift a car off her child if necessary. I get it.

This role affords us the opportunity for potential growth like we've likely never before known. It encourages us to look at ourselves closely, to see what changes need to be made in the interest of better parenting. Fears that had been repressed and successfully kept at bay often start to surface. Spiritual lessons previously learned have to be relearned within the context of motherhood and real love.

Clear intention towards personal evolution/growth, combined with discipline can help us to show and teach our children unconditional love – in action.

"I LOVE YOU"

What is "I love you"
If not a pledge of consistency?

What is "I love you"
If not a promise of respect and
unconditional positive regard?

What is "I love you"
If not a promise of unconditional forgiveness?

What is "I love you"
If not a statement of acceptance?

What is "I love you"
If not a cradle of perpetual
encouragement and support?

Why say "I love you"
If not resolved to WORK it?

Love is a verb. It requires action, not just talk. It is a consistent flow of right responses - or at least a consistent *attempt* at right responding. It is important to know what we mean when we say these words to our child. Love involves work and sacrifice and pushing through hard times and sometimes making unpopular decisions. But always, with love, the best interest of the child is the goal. So before giving in to reactive responses ask yourself the question: "What am I trying to do here? How can I demonstrate love in action?" Pause. Take a deep breath – and then respond. Let love inform your choices. Use love as fuel, as a balm, as a weapon against negativity and darkness. Make love your co-pilot.

A child who is consistently loved and cherished knows her value. He knows without a doubt that he has worth. This gift to our children trumps all others. Nothing material could ever take its place. Love costs nothing – but effort.

The warning-"Don't do it"

I know a woman who always warned of the perils and pitfalls of motherhood. "Don't do it," she admonished, half-smiling, half-serious "It's not worth it!" My gut reaction was at once "No! What's she talking about? She should savor the experience, cherish the little ones. She should just love them!"

Then, motherhood came my way and admittedly, the adjustment was more challenging than I anticipated. Heck, it was more challenging than I had ever *dreamed*. I hoped, feared, wept, angered, frustrated and wondered. I questioned my ability to love, to live up to the expectations. I prayed and waited. Then, seemingly all of a sudden, the reality "**NOT** a cross to bear" descended upon me and stayed. The awe, appreciation, wonder and challenge of it all became clear.

Now I understand my gut reaction to the woman's statement "It's not worth it." My reaction was at a soul level. **A soul which knew that a journey in unconditional love is ALWAYS worth it**. Yes, it is difficult, scary, unpredictable and potentially draining. But it is also a great opportunity to facilitate the development of another soul.

Is it for everyone? No! But the choice could be eased by knowledge of the process. No fairytales, no horror stories. Just the facts. The fact that motherhood is a process. A process which requires good intentions, discipline, commitment, strength and flexibility. A process which requires love to lubricate the daily work wheel. Without it, the movement is painful for both mother and child, each stage potentially agonizing, arduous and jarring. As is the case in most areas of life, it is our perception of a situation that determines its impact on our daily functioning. In the case of motherhood our perceptions also impact the hearts, minds and spirits of our offspring. Know what you believe and work towards the necessary alterations.

Children are perceptive. They will learn what we teach. We will teach what we believe.

Love is a multidimensional construct. It is not only a word. Love in action facilitates the physical, mental and psychological well - being of our offspring. It is not just hugs and kisses, but consistency, reliability and a strong resolve towards prioritizing the child's best interest. It requires a conscious choice to walk the talk. Love is WORK.

As each stage is completed, others emerge- sometimes with startling intensity. The "struggle" is ever present. Decide that the perception of "overwhelmed" is just that-a perception and cherish every moment of every day with the children. There is a responsibility which accompanies the decision to love. Yes, love requires discipline. Train your thoughts to accept that your responsibility is to assist their development in every way possible, to make their independence an ultimate goal.

There will be times when a calm, contented, dare I say "happy" feeling will descend upon you as you watch the children play. There will be times when it will occur to you that you are indeed doing a good job of the "motherhood thing." There will be times when you will allow yourself to completely fall into the moment, to transcend the daily and likely present chores and responsibilities yet unattended. Fall. Fall into those moments. They are energy-replenishing, they are uplifting, they are delicious. Your senses are alert, aware of their every noise, smile, imaginative thought. You can feel that "the children are happy." You can relax-for now.

REMIND YOURSELF THAT:

The children have come to rely on you
Let them feel your strength
Not your stress

The children have come to trust you
Let them feel secure
Not afraid

The children came here loving you
Let them feel your love
Not your fear

KIDS AS PURPOSE

In my darkest times, when fatigue and sadness descend upon me like an iron veil, it is always thought of "the kids" that instantly melts my armour, lights the dark and lifts the veil. They have become my greatest comfort, their well-being my singular focus. Oh my God! I *am* a mother. My purpose, at least immediately is to model unconditional love. This makes the daily decisions somewhat clearer – The choices more obvious.

In spite of the resistance to submit myself to their unconditional love (given and received) I find myself ensnared by their innocence, eyes wide, expecting the best of me – tired, frustrated, sad me. Although each time amazed, I rise to the occasion. This, after a quiet plea to the higher consciousness for help. Invariably, God answers and I carry on.

I must confess that motherhood has dragged me kicking and screaming into an "unconditional love" consciousness. In spite of my stubbornness and denial of the power, even existence of pure love, I have been unwittingly slapped in the face with the reality. Although I often wonder just how unwitting was my venture into motherhood. O.K. The Soul was ready – but not the Ego. I thank God for her nudging into a world which if left to my Ego –might still be unexplored – and what a pity!

I am also aware that some consider the purpose of reproduction a sort of old age insurance policy. The children are seen as potentially *useful*. Well, we all know about expectations. If elder care is the result, let it be because it is deserved, earned, not demanded or expected. While children can be a great source of comfort, their existence should not be for the sole purpose of *our* benefit.

Do not fool yourself into believing that they cannot intuit whether or not they are unconditionally loved or just an investment in *your* future.

WOULD YOU STILLLOVE ME IF???

Have you had the "Would you still love me if...?" conversation with your child? This was one of my defining moments. My son would run back and forth into my home office asking the question, each time with a more startling potential offence in the question [smile]. Each time that I responded "Yes, I would still love you", I could see the wheels turning as he tried to find some other reason why

I might stop loving him. "But would you still love me if...?" he continued.

Finally, I held his little face between my hands, looked him straight in the eye and said "There is nothing in the world that you could do to make me stop loving you." At once, his face softened. A feeling of pure satisfaction and contentment was evident in his little person. He had finally accepted this to be truth. He was loved. In a moment he knew his value and I knew I was up a creek!

My reassuring words were not just empty words. They were truth. A truth which brought to light my vulnerability and the realization that I was no longer in full control – as if I ever were. My heart was exposed.

NOW, my actions had to speak as loudly as my words.

NOW I had to remember what I was trying to communicate in every word and deed.

LOVE UNCONDITIONAL
IS THE PURPOSE. WHAT A RIDE!!

<u>Things I have learned at</u>
<u>my children's knees</u>

That love is ultimately the easier choice.

When the heart tugs against the rationalizations and other defenses of the ego – listen to the heart.

That my choices will one day mould their choices.

Since motherhood, I have become very cautious and hesitant to say the words "I love you" to others. These words should not be casually or carelessly expressed. The way I love my sons has shown me that [with the exception of my mother and brother] I had probably never before experienced true love.

That maybe I could reference that love experience with my children in dealing with others? Maybe my capacity to love has been increased. Maybe I could be more generally accepting of others?

I should share this new found capacity to love with my spouse? HMMM.

That my husband's love for our children has filled *me* up with more love for him.

Behaviours in my spouse that I previously believed were deliberate and intended to frustrate me might be genetic. LOL

That I *am* capable of unconditional love.

If necessary, I can push past seeming exhaustion and generate a crazy *second wind*– especially at Christmas and Birthday party times. Smile.

I have learned that my agenda for my sons is not necessarily their souls' agenda. I must frequently check in with Spirit on this issue.

I have learned that just a casual loving glance from one of the boys can send a ripple of calm through my entire being. A sense that everything is all right. But how so? With all of the responsibility that childrearing brings, with all of the ups and downs, the major adjustments, the unwanted changes - how so?

It is so because this is an experience of coming face to face with one of the purest forms of love, love from and for a child – *Your* children.

As your eyes lock with theirs, adoring, expectant of care, of unconditional love returned, you *know* that this is what it's all about. LOVE.

And you realize that the old clichés on the subject are based in fact.

I have learned that even when *their* love seems less than unconditional, Strive to make yours so

---

"MAMA"

Word of a child
Spoken in awe
Spoken in need
Expectant of care
To be counted on, to be there
Whether sad or tired or entrenched
In fear

Mama is, and Mama does
Mama tries to hold on tight
Mama cries and all you hear
Is the frightened beat of little hearts
Awaiting the return of love
So near

"Mama"
Word of love
NOT
A cross to bear

*I wrote this poem as a love letter to my
children, in a moment of spiritual clarity*

CHAPTER 4

||||||||||||||||||||||||||||||||||||||||||||||||||||||||||||||||||||||||||||||||||||||||||||||||||||||||||||

THE BIG DECISION

Disparaging remarks from women often came my way before I joined the "Mommy" club. Women would make comments about my being "a professional woman." Some would even ask; "So? How come *you* don't have any kids? What's the matter don't you *like* children? No time for kids huh?" Then the condescending, patronizing looks would follow. The message? If you do not have children something must be wrong with you. At best, something essential to your completion as a woman – is missing! The not so hidden message is that in spite of your other accomplishments in life, your lack of children means that you are not a *real* woman. I could barely restrain myself from grabbing them by the throat and shouting "What's it to YOU?" The audacity! The judgement! The suggestion that a childless woman is in some way less than those who reproduced, was infuriating.

Interestingly, only one or two would dare suggest that I might be in a better place without children. These were the brave honest few who were at some time entrenched in their own bout of mother frustration. They intimated that the elitism of the "For members only mother club" was just another way for suffering women to deny the same. This was a way to pretend that their new role was a badge of honour which somehow made them superior to their counterparts. Or maybe they had absolutely no difficulty adjusting to motherhood! Well good for them!

I observed another group of mothers. These women were able to calmly express frustration and agree that "this is not for everybody" while still maintaining optimism and a sense of fairness. They were less, if at all judgmental of the childless professional woman. These I believe were the women whose value was not defined by motherhood. In their minds, a person was not inherently more valuable if they had experienced the joys of the reproductive process. I salute these women. These are comrades.

There seems to be yet another "For members only club." These are the women who disparage motherhood and feel superior because they chose *not* to have children. They look at women with children as burdened and deprived of all that a woman today could accomplish for herself. Another exclusive group.

While I applaud the ability of some to make that no-child decision, there is no need for the often implied "superiority" and explicit condescension as a result of that choice.

Each choice is personal. Let us respect and honour an individual's decision about this life changing event. We are all different human beings, with varying goals and strengths as well as weaknesses. Regardless of into which category we fall, let us resolve to be respectful and honest with each other. Let us not judge each other. There is room for all.

When we feel guilty about our choice whatever that might be, we tend to overreact to other people's comments regarding that choice. We become defensive. Whatever your choice, there is no need to be apologetic. Recognize that it was a choice based on your own personal situation. Support and respect each other's choices.

Reproduction is only *one* way to learn about unconditional love. Life presents a myriad of opportunities for spiritual growth and a rise in consciousness.

IT IS NEITHER GOOD NOR BAD TO CHOOSE MOTHERHOOD IT IS JUST A CHOICE

The Conspiracy of Secrecy

Once you have become a mother, there is another decision to be made. Will you be honest or contribute to the "Conspiracy of Secrecy?" Why do so many women deny or at least minimize the difficulty of motherhood? One answer is the shock. Then there is the shame and guilt of having difficulty with such a *natural process*.

Over the years I have asked several women about this issue. This is a sample of the responses that were received.

- I couldn't believe how trapped I felt in my own home. The freedom to be able to leave whenever I wanted to was gone! I felt restricted. I felt that life would be very different if I didn't have children. I became impatient about doing what I had planned to do with my life after the children were grown and gone.
- Women do not talk about the difficulty because they don't want to appear less capable than they would like other women to believe – Competitive!

- With the first one, I was very young. Ignorance was bliss. When you have them at a young age it's like having a pet! It was very different with the second one, when I was more mature and aware of the responsibility and pressure.

- When I first came home from the hospital, I loved being a mom. Then reality set in. I didn't want to admit how hard it was.

- My big issue was time. You run out of time to do anything. I anticipated some of the difficulty. I was used to working 12- hour days in my profession. I could not *imagine* my life any busier than when I worked full time. But taking care of a child is a lot harder. At work I can say "I don't care, it's not *my* office." It's *Your* baby – so it's the responsibility.

- The daily routine is hard. There's no chance to slow down. Once they start walking and talking it's On! It's a whole new ball game.

- Fear – of something happening to the baby is the worst. I feel that many women do not admit how hard it is.

- Marriage is fine until you get pregnant. It's hard because he does not understand how you're feeling and he expects you to just *do it*. They [women] all talk about how horrible labour can be, but not afterwards. I felt absolutely helpless and trapped. I couldn't enjoy the baby because of all the responsibilities.

- Young people should be forced to read, to learn about this. Women are too closed. But what's to hide? Does it make me a better mother if I hide?

The one consistent theme was surprise at the difficulty. The solution? Information. Honesty from veteran mothers and others who understand that this is no easy task would facilitate a much smoother process of adjustment.

Honesty with yourself about your willingness and capacity to do the work, is essential. So let's be PROactive instead of REactive.

BEFORE making the big decision, consider the following;

Ask yourself: "Why do I want to become a mother? What is my intention? What are my expectations? Do I want to *get* something or *give* something by reproducing? Am I trying to please someone? Do I feel pressured? Do I even really want to be a mother? Be honest.

Make a resolution that any child you bear will not be at the mercy of your ignorance. While it is true that we cannot know everything and there is no *perfect* mother, there is no excuse for complete ignorance.

Learn about yourself, as much as you can - and again be honest. What do you believe? What do you assume about motherhood and life in general? What changes could you make? Look your flaws straight in the eye. The more clarity, the less likely you are to be blindsided by issues that might arise.

Learn about the responsibility of motherhood. Talk to others.

Expect constant challenge to your emotional constancy and resilience. Clarify your expectations. Identify ways to refuel before the tank is empty.

Be prepared to grow. Don't expect "easy."

Start to assemble your village of supporters. These do not have to be blood relations. They do not even have to be other mothers. Support can come from some surprising places. Friends, neighbours, can all be helpful in the adjustment.

Get ready for BIG LOVE.

YOU HAVE A RIGHT TO YOUR CHOICE WHATEVER THAT MIGHT BE THERE IS NO NEED TO DEFEND A DECISION TO/NOT TO REPRODUCE

After making the decision

<u>REMEMBER</u>

Do not hold on too tightly to control.

Admit to the difficulty if that is your experience. Do not live in denial. Ask for and accept help.

Communicate appreciation of help – from anyone.

Just because someone has not had children does not mean that they cannot provide helpful advice. Sometimes an outsider's view is the clearest. An unbiased perspective can be more original and less emotional.

In my experience, men can be very practical and solution-oriented. Maybe the husband's recommendations could be met with less disdain? It doesn't matter if he does not understand how you feel. He might still have reasonable solutions and advice to offer. Be open. This is survival mode.

If you need to cry, do it in the shower – You're wet anyway.

Celebrate your strength. You've made it this far. Look at your reflection in the mirror and offer words of encouragement and affirmation.

If we want things to change we have to accept the responsibility to make them change.

This too shall pass. Children *do* grow up.

Surrender to the wonder of the role.

Make flexibility a motto.

ENJOY THE NEST FULL

The decision-older women

I have had the dubious honour of having children later in life. I knew what it was like to be free to use my time and energy as I saw fit. I was at a place in life where I had accomplished the academic and professional goals that I had set. I had done a lot of personal work in the area of spirituality. So I thought that in spite of the absence of close family members, I could breeze through this new stage in my life. Ha! What a joke!

In addition to the already discussed difficulty with the process, there was the additional issue of my age. Let's not forget that as we approach 40-ish years, we often begin to experience hormonal fluctuations which could catapult us into unfamiliar bouts of distress. Just when we need as much emotional stability as we can get, perimenopause rears its ugly head. We must therefore learn to differentiate between the sources of our emotional regulation challenges. I hate to say it, but sometimes our perceived distress *is* hormonally sourced. Let us not jump to blame all of our emotions on the newness of motherhood. This could just be *one* of the contributing factors. In spite of our youthful offspring and the joy of having finally reproduced, we cannot forget that time forges on and our bodies are changing. Do not allow fluctuating hormones to rob you of precious time with your children.

Obvious disadvantages aside, having children later also has its benefits. Life experience and wisdom come to mind. Older women have had the opportunity to experience more freedom and might be less likely to resent the monopolization of their time. It is also possible that financial stresses might be less. These all help to decrease the amount of energy that could be wasted in worry over these issues.

There are pros and cons of making the decision at any age. No one time is perfect in all areas. Again, it is a very personal decision.

Horrible Thoughts

Let's get one thing straight. We all are capable of so- called *horrible* thoughts. Do not indulge in excessive self-criticism because thoughts such as "I would be better off if I had not made this decision" might occur. The brain automatically tries to find its way out of tight spots. Some of the *resolutions* that occur to us might be startling. But we shouldn't immediately panic.

Thoughts of abandonment of responsibility do not mean that a person will definitely behave in maladaptive or even dangerous ways. But everything is information. If these thoughts or feelings persist or intensify, it is a message to pay attention, talk to our closest people and seek professional help.

It often takes the occurrence of frightening thoughts to push us into the realization that we are depleted in emotional resources – that we have reached our limit.

They are unique

Children fill a space in a way that nothing else can- that no one else can - Not in the same way.

Even in the happiest of marriages, there is sometimes a need to draw the children close, as comfort, as encouragement. Just mom and the kids. Perhaps their innocent, uncomplicated, unconditionally loving demeanor somehow replenishes our energy cup and renews our resolve to forge ahead. I have found that in the darkest, most frightening of times, a smile or little voice can reach down into my soul and dig out the seemingly last bit of strength. Whatever the particular experience of motherhood, the combination of joy and fear and sadness and satisfaction - is incomparable!

Whether or not one decides to take the mother-trip, does not alter the fact that this is one unique and often surprising journey. This is a journey with twists and turns like no other. It is an opportunity for increased awareness and spiritual evolution. It is a journey to a rise - of consciousness.

CHAPTER 5

SACRED TRUST

A Trust is a responsibility placed in the hands of one entity [the Trustee] by another [the Trustor], for the benefit/protection of a third [the Beneficiary]. In legal settings this usually refers to assets such as land or money. The assumption is that the trustee will at all times have the best interest of the beneficiary in mind if not at heart. Consistent right action is assumed and to be expected from the trustee. The characterization of motherhood as a Sacred Trust has been very helpful to my "Big Picture" perspective. In this scenario, the child has been entrusted to the mother by God, for safe keeping. I see the purpose as fostering the evolution of another soul. There is an accountability here which may or may not resonate with some. I suppose it is dependent upon your belief system.

That a child is a sacred trust can be a quickly re-orienting thought on dark days of fatigue. It can help us to remember that there is a purpose higher than the immediate one. These little trusts are the hope of the future. While our immediate feelings/ perceived needs might at the time appear of primary importance, there is a much larger concern than ourselves. We are part of a caretaking force that is blessed by virtue of its wondrous responsibility. Reverence for the responsibility seems appropriate.

These little charges are on loan to us by a larger Force. Let us focus on providing roots, wings and always love. They are not our possessions. We are their facilitators. If we are to be well-functioning mothers we must resolve to consistently acknowledge the importance of the task. Regardless of the efforts of others to minimize this role, daily practice of those self-statements which affirm its importance is in order.

It is encouraging and comforting to think of being in a partnership with some higher Force, some omniscient being - God. Imagine the help that is available if requested. Since we cannot do everything well all of the time, it behooves us to surrender to that Force that can. Ask assistance from the Trustor. After all, the well- being of the child is at the very least just as important to that higher being, as it is to us. Also, that big picture that we might strive to maintain is very clear to the Source.

In order to benefit from this assistance once requested, we must learn to listen *to* and *for* the direction. We are often so busy entertaining the ramblings of the Ego, that we fail to hear the direction that we seek. It is also possible for us to assume [and fear] that our personal childhood challenges might repeat in our child's life. We therefore anticipate and almost *plan* how we would handle this eventuality. So instead of paying close attention to the individual and unique needs of *this* particular child, we set about to provide them with what *we* need/needed. Of course there are universal basic needs such as food, shelter, clothing etc. which occupy most of our attention. But there is nothing more wonderful for a child than the frequent receipt of their mother's undivided, loving attention. Attention that is focused on learning the unique needs of *this* child. This is a real gift that is always appreciated by the little darlings. It communicates to them that they are valued, important and special.

In order to provide this kind of care, it is expected that we can be present, *in the moment* as they often say nowadays. This brings us full circle to the need for the mother to take as much care of herself as is reasonably possible. In the face of fatigue and busy-ness it is difficult to stop and smell the roses with your child. But it has long lasting positive effects on the development of this precious trust.

BE QUIET!!!

Be quiet! God is talking! Have you ever had the experience of a noisy, unrelenting dialogue between you and yourself? It usually goes like this: "Oh God! I'm so tired, I don't know what to do.....my spouse doesn't understand, this is so hard, I'm a horrible mother....please help me God!" And the dialogue goes on. No pause for a breath, no pause for a word of hope to slip in, no pause for God to answer. Be quiet, God wants to answer you but you won't shut up. Filter out that background noise that is you. Try this in the middle of a complaint session with yourself or spouse/partner. Just say "STOP! God is talking." See how you immediately begin to calm down. And then listen – *truly* listen.

ENJOY THE NEST FULL

In the early stages of motherhood I often muttered under my breath "Empty nest syndrome indeed! I just can't wait to be there." I was sure that I would not experience any anxiety, much less suffering at the emptying of my nest. But these were words spoken in the heat of frustration and fatigue. As time passed and the bond deepened, I practiced surrender and lovingly accepted this precious responsibility. The words "Sacred Trust" emerged in my consciousness. I slowly and somewhat reluctantly began to understand the potential pain of an empty nest – of my sons no longer needing and depending on their mother. I simultaneously became awe struck and humbled by the Trustor's implied faith in my ability to positively impact the evolution of another soul.

So within the context of *Sacred Trust*, I resolved to enjoy the nest full – to slowly breathe in and out as I stroked their heads at bedtime, to marvel at the miracles that lay before me. "God! I still cannot believe that I am someone's mother!" I resolve to provide them with pleasant memories and a clear sense of their value which could ultimately assist them in navigating this existence. When they reflect on their childhood, let them recall love, focused attention and a clear knowledge that "My mother loved me."

SAVOUR THE MOMENTS WHEN.....

Just a touch of his little cheek against yours, a loving smile, words spoken "I adore you mommy. You are my soul!" infuse your every sense with a peace and joy that is matchless.

You are quiet with your child(ren) and you manage to narrow your focus to "now." These moments are far too rare. These moments are refueling. These moments remind us of God.

In these moments if we listen very closely, we can hear the beating of our hearts, of the child's heart and then their beating in unison.

In these moments we know that we are indeed one soul, just split apart – for now.

MANTRA FOR DAYS OF EXHAUSTION AND DESPAIR....

As I am from "The Source" so is my child sourced from me.

Although apart from me, still a part *of* me.

I will love him as God loves me – Selflessly.

I will be there when needed. No thought of selfish needs or desires.

No feelings of deprivation. No experience of resentment.

My perceived needs are fulfilled by my fulfillment of her needs.

What I give to my child I therefore give to myself.

Just patience.

Just love.

Just sacred benefit from choosing me to be "Trustee."

CHAPTER 6

||||||||||||||||||||||||||||||||||||||||||||||||||||||||||||||||||||||||||||||||||||||||||||||||||||||||||||||||||

ADJUSTMENT

At the risk of stating the obvious, life is a series of stages and changes demanding adjustment. But what do we mean when we say *adjustment*? The old adage to "Bloom where you're planted" comes to mind. If we recall our high school biology class, the term *adaptation* was used to describe ways in which a species adjusts to changes in its environment. The degree of adaptation accomplished could be measured by how well the species learned to function, survive and multiply in this new environment. In layman's terms, it had to get used to or accept the changes in order to survive as well as thrive.

The term *adjustment* has been used interchangeably with adaptation. Any demand placed on a person to cope with the challenges and changes of life often requires an adjustment [alteration, change] in thought, emotions and behavior. In order for the adjustment to be adaptive, the changes that are made should facilitate the best functioning of the individual. The changes should result in not only survival, but flourishing. In the case of motherhood, we have already established that best functioning of the mother is a major facilitator of best functioning of the child.

Individual differences in personality, intellectual profile, life experiences etc. will all inform our capacity for effectively dealing with significant life changes. But to whatever extent we are capable, we are obligated to make our best effort in this life-changing role. We do not have to be perfect, but there are certain basics that could be helpful.

The admission of difficulty, awareness of the impact of stress and use of discipline as we navigate motherhood are all potentially facilitative of a good adjustment. Reminding ourselves that we are not alone in our struggle, that we must be efficient in the use of our precious energy and that we must be willing to honestly look at ourselves should be recurring mantras.

However, the *acceptance* of change [or at least the *intention* towards acceptance] is of paramount importance and an ultimate goal. Acceptance is a state which usually results from a great deal of psychological work. It often emerges after the more emotionally distressing part of an adjustment process. We can acknowledge that life has drastically changed following reproduction, accept it as fact and resolve to move with the flow – or we can resist. But the changes *will* continue.

In the interest of energy efficiency and right acting, which approach intuitively and rationally makes the most sense?

GRIEF

What specifically are these changes to which we are supposed to adjust? We know of the obvious ones such as lack of sleep. But what about the less obvious, potentially more significant changes? It has been my observation that in some ways, motherhood demands an awareness of and eventual adjustment to loss. Let's be honest. There is a grieving process which often goes unnoticed. What are we grieving? The following are some of the *possible* perceived losses resulting from this change in status.

- Loss of freedom
- Loss of independence

- Loss of career
- Loss of body shape/tone
- Loss of personal dreams and aspirations
- Loss of rose - coloured view of spouse

These perceived losses warrant an appropriate amount of time in your adjustment process. There are various emotions which could occur in response to any kind of loss. From shock, to anger to eventual acceptance, this roller coaster ride of emotions presents a serious challenge for some women. The identification of the process as grief, could be helpful. Resistance of the fact that there is loss, could delay acceptance of the new role. Let's not be stubborn. Do not forget the importance of dedication to reality or the truth. Let go of the lost dream in its old form. Be willing to adjust the dream and intend towards acceptance of the new. The acknowledgement that there is a lost ideal, pushes us to re-establish more realistic and hopefully adaptive ways of being. It also makes way for far more wondrous possibilities. As some dreams die, better ones emerge.

We cannot deny the wonder of love unconditional.

CHANGE THE THOUGHTS

Many are unaware of the background self-statements that constantly play in our heads. The identification and alteration of these thoughts can be a challenging and lengthy process. However, if we are to consciously move towards changes in ourselves that improve our mothering we should strive to identify some of the more prominent counter - productive thoughts, kick them to the curb and replace them with ones that keep us on the right track. Openness to honest self-reflection can be helpful here. A shortcut is to ask people who know you well, to identify things that they hear you frequently say. Ask them what they think you believe. The results could be all at once shocking and illuminating.

Once we have *some* clarity about which thoughts are self-sabotaging, we must try to be flexible in our approach. Flexibility is a very useful tool in the adjustment to change. It frees us to generate more creative solutions in problem solving. It eases the stress of daily responsibilities. Why do chores always have to be done in the same way, every time, right away? Why can't we sometimes go with the flow? Likely because we are telling ourselves that we have to be perfect in this mother role – as many other women *seem* to be.

Again, the curse of secrecy and expectation raises its ugly head. The less rigid we become with unimportant tasks, the more consistently we can focus our limited energy on the much more important task of being present with the children. When we model flexibility, the children are more likely to learn it earlier in life.

TO BE UNDERSTOOD

"I just want to be understood!" The cry of many mothers. I believe that for many, feeling understood is not only an emotional need, but also intellectually necessary in order for them to move forward along that adjustment path. It is as though a switch is thrown, some mental trace of "relief" is laid down and one can almost feel the release in the brain as it is declared "So! You *know* what I mean?"

Of course, we could also get stuck in that need to be understood – keeping ourselves back emotionally, making no tangible changes in our daily behaviour because we chant "No one understands!" While feeling understood is immediately gratifying and potentially facilitative of emotional progress, we must not spend an eternity waiting for it to occur. We must not become immobilized because "No one understands!" Let's face it. This could be a very convenient way of avoiding real change, of not accepting responsibility for our internal environment.

As long as we remain unique and individual, it is impossible for anyone to "truly and completely" understand anyone else. Even people with identical physical or psychiatric diagnoses do not *completely* understand what the other experiences. We each process information in novel ways. So it is somewhat pointless to spend precious time lamenting the belief that you are misunderstood. Reassurance and encouragement could appear in the most unlikely places, so remain open to its appearance in any form and from any source.

Yes, even childless individuals could be potential sources of genuine empathy and practical advice. After all, it is not necessary to have a disease in order to find its cure!

Throw off the defensiveness and condescension and be willing to give up your membership in the "misunderstood mother" club. Remember the immediate goal here is survival. The long-term goal is adaptive adjustment. Yes - Even if it means taking advice from those childless (and might I add, often well-rested) women.

Emotional control has its place and importance in the process of adjustment. At times it is better to suspend the emotions in favour of rational thoughts, choices and behaviours. Do what's necessary to first survive and then thrive. When in your calmest state, ponder alternatives that might be more adaptive and long lasting. At all costs, have faith in your ability to successfully manoeuver this journey.

Learn to interrupt your own *babble* of negativity. Say STOP!

Find a positive alternative statement and babble that instead.

Learn that if it's on your plate, it's meant to be part of your meal. It might not be the delicious, easy to swallow dessert. It might be the vegetables, the nonpalatable brussels sprouts. But we all know that the vegetables serve us the best in the end.

<u>REMEMBER</u>

In order to successfully cope with the sacred trust of motherhood, increased self-awareness is required. Clarity of your goal is paramount. Making the child's best interest the priority simplifies many choices. And in every moment, there is a choice.

I recall the well-recounted story of the grandfather who was instructing his grandson in the ways of the world. He explained that there are two wolves inside of us fighting for power, one good and one evil. [I characterize these as light and darkness]. The grandson asks "Which one wins?" the wise grandfather answers "Whichever one we feed." If we are honest, we know in the moment whether we are feeding light or darkness.

As we make the adjustment to motherhood, we could pass through a host of experiences. Hopefully, we get to a place where loving choice becomes automatic. We see that our present efforts, sacrifices and struggles could provide a foundation for resiliency in our children. When we feed the light wolf, we are also feeding the child.

As is often the case in life, our greatest challenges bring us the greatest reward. This is profoundly so of motherhood.

The adaptation to the change could be surprisingly satisfying, successful and productive of incredible offspring. This could be your contribution to humanity.

**WHERE THERE IS TIME THERE
CAN BE CHANGE
BE PATIENT
LET THE PROCESS MARINATE**

**PERHAPS MOTHERHOOD IS
YOUR AREA OF GENIUS**

CHAPTER 7

|||||||||||||||||||||||||||||||||||||||||||||||||||||||||||||||||||||||||||||||||||||||||||||||||||||||||||||||||||||||

SPIRITUAL JOURNEY

Every challenge with which we are presented provides a potential occasion for personal growth. We all have lessons to learn and contributions to make in our lives. No one lesson is unimportant in terms of spiritual evolution. In my opinion, parenthood provides a wonderful training ground. It is also an opportunity for us to mould another soul, to pass on what we have learned and to ultimately contribute to that essential and long - awaited critical mass of evolved beings. So each choice made in motherhood is not just for ourselves but the rest of the world. Teach your child about the law of attraction, that the universe is supportive and miraculous. But first, teach it to yourself.

What we believe is where we live. I believe that life is a brief visit of our spirit to the carnal plane. A journey of our true being to a place of experience and hopefully evolution. Motherhood is potentially a huge part of that journey. Childhood is also a part of the journey. The mother/child relationship is a journey towards both the giving as well as receiving of love. It is an opportunity to experience the workings of unconditional love - to feel its power. It is a glorious journey to a *potential* rise in consciousness. I say *potential* because a deliberate/ intentional decision has to be made towards this goal if it is to be achieved.

I cannot count the number of times in my life as a parent when it was helpful and necessary to stop and ask myself: "What is my goal. What *is* my goal?" before responding to my child. Self-instructions to "choose the light wolf" or "just choose light" or "provide roots then wings" all simplified and made clear the most proactive response. At the very least it afforded a pause before making a *reactive* response. While we might not all subscribe to a spiritual Big Picture, we must surely agree that the highest development of the child is a basic goal. While focusing on their physical and intellectual development, make some room for the spiritual. Note that I did not say *religious* but *spiritual* development. This opens the door for that connection to a higher power in *any* way possible, not just through an organized doctrinal setting.

ENLISTING SPIRITUAL HELP

There is a simple utility in focus on a spiritual big picture. In times of difficulty, this big picture can foster efficient use of your precious energy. In the interest of efficiency, I have moved much closer to God. There is now a really friendly ease with which we communicate. No time to kneel. No time to meditate. No time to...... But even in the midst of chaos and bewilderment [perhaps especially so] there is a calm, reassuring presence. A presence more real to me than the one previously *summoned* through more formal activities of prayer and meditation. I now find myself engaged in continuous dialogue with a force so powerful and omniscient that even in the midst of my "overwhelmed-ness" there is contentment and a faith in the process. The Big Picture renewed and reviewed.

Getting to God is a lot easier than we often choose to believe. Yes. It is a choice. And again, we do not all have to subscribe to the same version of this Force, Source, Energy or whatever makes you comfortable. But one thing is certain. Acknowledgement that there *is* spiritual help available, and surrendering to its wisdom can be very helpful to both mother and child. We can ask that Power to show us our strength and to open our senses to the ever - present guidance that is all around us. You don't necessarily have to believe this in the beginning. Just fake it till you make it. Remember that what we tell ourselves is driving the bus.

Fear is my definition of the Devil. It is the most powerful and negative force in this world. Fear blocks creativity and miracles. It not only blocks miracles that occur outside of ourselves but also those within. Fear of the responsibility of motherhood, our ability to cope, finances, safety of the children, all inhibit clarity and effective problem solving. It can also drag us away from the "Forest" aspect of our lives. It makes us forget that the goal is long-term, and throws us back into the mindset of urgency. It makes us forget that spiritual support is ever present. But we can fight back with Faith. We can fight back with the certainty that we can generate what is needed in order to shine in this role. Dare to be optimistic, to be positive. Dare to enjoy the new responsibility of motherhood.

I recall one morning when particularly fearful, I reached a place of deep surrender. I pleaded "God! Please take over today. Whatever You are, make

Me." All at once I felt relief. But I also realized that I had recently made the same request, repeatedly. Then it descended upon me, the profound truth that God *does not have a memory problem!!* [*Smile*]

It is not necessary to repeat over and over again that you are so stressed, need help etc. At least it is not necessary to a positive outcome. It might feel necessary to you because you believe that each time you ask for spiritual help, it somehow increases the chance of the need being met. No. All it does is remind *you* of the need. Don't nag God. He knows your need.

SPIRITUAL SUPPORTERS

Spiritual supporters, [whether incarnate or otherwise] are part of your "village." I had a dream once, where I could actually see an auditorium - like room, filled with worker- bee- type angelic supporters. These were *my* personal workers. No one else could see them but me. They were busily working to facilitate my success on this earthly plane. It was amazing. Of course, it was at the same time daunting and encouraging to realize that God thought I needed *that* much help!!

I have come to refer to this group of helpers as my SPIRIT POSSE. I find it humbling and amusing when I think of them tirelessly in my corner, unconditionally loving, non-judgemental and always working for my spiritual growth. Whether real or not, this dream served a practical purpose. It provided me the much-needed comfort, reassurance and encouragement to soldier on. It reminds me that although not always visible, help is near. Help for me is help for my children. So I am grateful.

We have been told by many spiritual leaders through the ages that what we can sense with five senses is only a fraction of what actually exists. One of my favourite authors Gary Zukav describes a more enlightened "multisensory" being whose vision is unlimited. Perhaps unknowingly, we have all had multisensory experiences.

Have you ever felt as though you were at the end of your rope, asked/begged for spiritual assistance and marveled at the outcome? Have you never sensed the immediate and powerful presence of spiritual helpers? It does not matter whether the mechanism of assistance is through another human being, an occurrence/event or seemingly "spiritual" helpers. It is all miraculously the same – an answer to your cry.

To my Spirit Posse I say:

THANK YOU FOR YOUR TIRELESS EFFORTS ON MY BEHALF

In the final analysis, we are responsible for our own behavior and level of consciousness. If we choose to live this life without thought and reflection then we are making the road more difficult for our beloved offspring. After all, they do watch and tend to mimic what we do. So show them strength. Show them that *suffering* is almost always unnecessary. Teach them by your actions that Heaven can be now and here. The parent-child relationship reflects that of the Source and humanity. While the ultimate goal is the ability to function independently of the parent, there should always be a connection and accessibility to the parent.

THE FALLACY OF CONTROL

Try not to worry about being completely ready for this role. There is no such thing. Every experience is in some way unique. The belief that being in control of all is necessary and good, is misleading and inaccurate. It is the work of the Ego, not the

Spirit. We must free ourselves from the expectation of having it all under control before we even consider motherhood. Because let me tell you, it'll become clear soon enough, that this pursuit of control is a major ingredient in the frustration pie! More importantly, it is a distraction from the Big Picture.

We cannot be capable and competent in every sphere of life, at every moment, under every circumstance. We are human. Learn to love some disarray, both in external surroundings as well as your internal environment. Feeling overwhelmed and in "sensory overload" does not mean that you are incompetent, does not mean that you are crazy. It is a message – a clear communication that better organization, adjusted expectations and definitely more sleep – are in order. It nudges us towards mobilizing our spiritual helpers. Spend the energy on the latter, not on self-recrimination. Remember, the child must not become collateral damage.

"THE MASTER SOUL IS CONSTANT"

When I read this statement several years ago in *The Quiet Mind* [Sayings of White Eagle] I immediately experienced an overwhelming feeling of clarity. The simplicity of this statement was riveting. Here was a mantra with which I could not only identify, but easily access when teetering on despair. Coupled with the memory of my mother and grandmother's frequently repeated words "The race is not for the swiftest, but for he who can endure" I finally had access to powerful statements which could reach back into my psyche and hook positive emotions. To be constant or at least *attempt* to be constant. Yes! That gives some clarity. This is a journey of ENDURANCE! The HOW of maintaining that clarity is another matter. Here, work is required.

The nurturance of another human spirit is an honourable exercise. I chose the word *exercise* to stress both the need to expend energy as well as the need for repetition and constant practice. We cannot instantly arrive at constancy of mind and action without some sweat and often much tears. We cannot be constant without discipline. There's that *magic bullet* word again.

Any spiritual path is rife with struggle and challenge. Each step along the path is eased and facilitated by disciplined practice. We have all seen the wonderful results that are possible when individuals persist against odds, persevere and practice a skill diligently and *religiously*. Accomplishments of

Olympians come to mind. With time, the skill becomes an automatic response, performed with apparent ease as well as consistency.

Should we not apply these well proven approaches and techniques to the most important job of all? Should we not be willing to sacrifice immediate gratification for long term benefit to the child? Enjoy the journey, the nest full, the challenges of spirit that are sent and indeed *called* our way. We miss too much of the meat of the process if engrossed in urgency for outcome.

It is widely known that children thrive in environments of consistency, predictability and unconditional love. In order for them to receive constantly what they need, the parent must strive towards constancy of spirit.

SELF-CRITICISM

"I hate myself when I'm impatient, when I snap and I see the crestfallen look on those innocent little faces. Then, I begin to feel guilty, sad, angry, depressed – too tired to care! How on earth did my life turn into such a storm of emotions? Oh Yes! I reproduced!!!"

Sound familiar? You do not have to be so self-deprecating. Many women have the same experience. They question their capability and inner fortitude. They see themselves as unable to easily maintain that emotional constancy that we always hear about. But like any quest towards a particular goal, there will be obstacles, challenges, self-doubt and yes FEAR.

The good news, is that these are merely potential stepping stones to real growth, to a rise in consciousness. Yes, we will experience negative emotions along the way but with each repeated choice to be non -reactive and focused on the ultimate goal we one day realize that we have become less affected by external events. This day does not just appear out of nowhere however. If we are to arrive at "calm" we must cultivate right thinking, especially about our own uniqueness and value, our efficacy and power. The Big Picture ever present in our mind and heart.

We are not all at that lofty spiritual level which allows a constant giving of self, without negative side effects. That is a personal goal for many – but all in good time. On this journey of growth, we must embrace and celebrate each stage – even the resentful, angry, frustrated and tired stages.

Challenges provide opportunity for growth and evolution, for positive and adaptive change. Resist the impulse towards self-blame and recrimination when you perform in less than *supermom* ways. That only wastes time, energy and decreases creative problem solving. The responsibility of motherhood is a challenge like no other. It takes time and effort but you can become better able to cope. Believe and expect it. Demand it of yourselves. Then one day – growth!

WHEN THE EGO IS CERTAIN THAT IT *KNOWS*, THINK AGAIN AND CONSULT THE SPIRIT

AND WHEN YOU FALTER

That motherhood is a potential path to spiritual evolution descended upon me relatively early in the process. In an attempt at accessing my best, I asked myself two questions;

A. What do I want most for my sons?

With time and much effort, the answer that emerged was: *That they learn those lessons contracted by their spirit – in this lifetime, with minimal suffering. That they rise and continue to rise in consciousness. That they know the answer to the question "Who am I?"* The benefit of this approach in terms of sustaining emotional constancy and remaining in the Big Picture frame of mind, cannot be over emphasized.

B. What is the ultimate goal of *my* life?

This answer was more easily accessible: *To counteract with light [in ways large and small], any and all darkness which crosses my life path. To ease the suffering of others, show them their value and become constant.* Easier said than done! But at least I had a goal right? [smile] Ultimately, I also realized that my goal for my sons was also my goal for myself – to know and remember *Who I am*. So we journey together.

If you can answer these two questions you will find that your choices and decisions are consistently informed. Keep these goals in mind always. In every situation, through each moment of challenge, frustration, desperation, always return to the question: "Am I feeding the light or fueling darkness?" The right response is much more likely to become clear.

It might not be the ego's choice [which is often sourced from fear/darkness] but the spirit will tug you in the *Light* direction - the direction of spiritual evolution for both the parent as well as the child.

LEARN TO LISTEN TO THE SPIRIT THE MESSAGE IS OFTEN SOFT EMANATING FROM A GUT OR HEART LEVEL

ENCOURAGEMENT

The daily trudge towards our
chosen goal can be arduous
And apparently futile

But with each inch of the journey conquered,
we slowly approach that which seemed elusive

Despite the circuitous nature of the road,
it ALWAYS leadS to HOME

(Your friend)

[written for a dear friend in a dark time]

ON A PERSONAL NOTE

My mother died when I was 13 years old and my brother almost 15. She was 36 years old and the love of our lives. We watched her suffer for more than one year before she crossed over. It was the most gut wrenching and life-changing event for both of us. However, we had the good fortune to have been raised by a woman who epitomized motherhood. In spite of our challenges throughout this lifetime, we have always known at the core that we are valuable - and this, "because our mother loved us." We knew that we were her priority.

We were robbed of the opportunity to spend adult years with our mother but she is ever present in our hearts. The unconditional love that she showed was a model for my own relationship with my sons. Of course she was not perfect, but in those first 13 years of my life I knew that she would sacrifice all for her children - and without a hint of resentment or martyrdom. I loved her intensely. We had a bond like no other.

As a defense against potentially losing my mind I responded to her death with calm detachment. I told myself that I could handle "anything" and actually proved that quite well over the years. I found that I could maintain sufficient emotional distance from anyone in order to avoid that deep feeling of attachment and ultimately [potentially] of loss. That is, of course, until I became a mother.

Admittedly, the overwhelming, unconditional love that I experienced for my baby was not immediately acknowledged. After more than two and a half decades of practiced detachment, one could not expect change overnight. Oh but what a wonderful change! As time passed and my son and I looked into each other's eyes, that first love that I felt for my mother came sweeping back. I knew I was hooked! I knew that my defenses had not only been obliterated, but were somehow no longer necessary! As the birth of my second son approached I feared that I would not have sufficient love left for another child. After all, how could I possibly love TWO individuals this way?

GOOD NEWS! LOVE HAS NO LIMITS!! Once more, my heart opened.

I was quite willing to surrender to *this* love.

Partially as a result of my clinical training in Psychology and partially due to intuition, I knew that generating a clear goal for this new role and greatest of responsibilities was fundamental to any success. So I asked myself "What am I trying to do here? Is it just providing for physical needs, education, etc.?" That did not seem enough. I decided that I wanted the children to be "gentlemen"- to have respect, integrity, good behavior etc.- but still not enough! AHA! I had it! I want to assist them in the accomplishment of their spiritual goals - those goals chosen by their spirits for this lifetime.

My own spiritual study and journey had taught me that being loving and living consciously, in awareness, towards spiritual evolution, was the ultimate goal. I wanted to teach them to emulate the characteristics of nonjudgment, sensitivity and sharing. I wanted them to know that we are all connected, each a small spark from that energy that sourced us. Sounded like a tall order but it made it clear that I would have to be accountable for my actions and willing to accept the challenge if I wanted to teach in the most effective manner -i.e. by example.

I would have to be willing to admit to and correct *my* mistakes.

Enter anxiety. Performance anxiety. Questions about my own ability to maintain this level of "right acting" were many and frequently occurring. However, when I found myself about to lose it or act impulsively, it was very helpful to ask myself "What are you trying to do here? OK. Teach nonjudgment, show sensitivity" or whichever lesson was appropriate at the time.

I often stated my goals out loud so that they too would understand my reasons for certain responses and choices. As a matter of fact, it became a bit of a joke around the house and the boys would roll their eyes and say "We know, you're trying to raise gentlemen!"

"Well, at least we *all* know the goal" - would be my response. LOL

I have feared, panicked, prayed, begged God and surrendered. Through it all, there has always been this calm, constant, nonreactive Observer – little did I know that this was also me – Consciousness *In Waiting*.......

<u>PERSONAL MANTRAS</u>

Fear is the enemy. Replace it with FAITH and certainty.

Where FAITH lives, fear cannot dwell.

What you feed grows. What you starve dies. Feed the LIGHT.

Take back control from the reactive Ego. Let Spirit drive the bus. Ego and Personality are just passengers.

With each choice ask yourself: "Is this the Light or Dark Wolf directing my actions?" You know which one to choose.

What you do not like in others, Correct in yourself.

What you give you will CERTAINLY receive. So the choice is obvious.

Our lives must not be reduced to a series of reactions to the behaviour of others or any particular circumstances – external or internal.

We should hold our focus on the Big Picture – climbing that ladder of spiritual evolution towards the state of a Master Soul.

CALM IS WHERE THE POWER LIES

AFTERWORD

This work was birthed from a need to self-soothe. To my surprise the impulse to record my experience was effective and there was soon a plethora of paper strategically placed around the house, available for quick grasp and reading in times of desperation. [Smile] These times were becoming so frequent that organization of the notes into one easily accessible blue and white plastic file box seemed an efficient move.

As the years passed the notes grew and I noticed that they were self- instructional, reminding me to practice what I preach. I was forced to become aware of the tendency towards self-absorption and the resultant emotional distress. It is important to learn to recognize this tendency, label it, put it into perspective and then resolve to remember that "it's not all about you." Emotions are heightened in the early days of motherhood. It is unrealistic to expect that everyone will acquiesce to your needs.

But it is essential to realize that as you strive to do your best there is an underlying process of adjustment through which you are being ushered.

Awareness of this process, acceptance of it and determination to make the adjustment adaptive, all work to reduce the difficulty and improve the outcome.

To say that motherhood can be a struggle is an understatement. To say that the struggle is wonderful, full of wonder, is truth. It can take several years of motherhood before the consistent appreciation of the journey develops. But what better use of time than in the facilitation of another human being's spiritual journey? As unconditionally loving as they are, these little beings have the capacity to enflame any flicker of the same that might be present in the parent. A child's love, pure and simple, innocently expressed could defuse even the most stressed of us.

Let us take the time to bask in the pure adoration of our children. Let us stop and explore how it feels when our child says "I love you" and file that away for future reference. Let us place that warm memory in our stress busting arsenal to be retrieved and utilized in times of emotional distress. Say to yourself "This child loves me - ME! My best is what he expects and my best is what she deserves."

Decide to be mindful of their love for you, even if you cannot maintain mindfulness of your love for them in every moment. Consciously intend and decide to behave in loving ways, in *all* ways. Note that this is a process. Like it or not we must have faith in the process and strive to do our best.

When I discovered my first pregnancy the ego threw me into a tailspin of shock, disbelief, confusion, helplessness, uncontrollability and unpredictability. Fear gripped my mind. But the Soul knew the goal. The Soul intended towards my self-proclaimed decision to foster the spiritual development of one other than my own. To my later delight, my Soul took over and kicked me into the greatest adventure of my life. MOTHERHOOD. That opportunity to experience unconditional love, given and received. I was catapulted into the journey to a rise in consciousness.

Judging from my initial response to pregnancy one might challenge that it was at all Soul-driven. But as we all know the ego can be a formidable opponent. Enter the doubts; "But I'm 38 years old! What about my career? My own mother died at 36! What if *I die and leave my children alone – to suffer – without mother love?? I Can't do this! God help me.*" And She has.

The early days of doubt have melted away, as has my heart. This is not to say that daily struggle with responsibility and self-control has completely vanished. To the contrary, the struggle remains, but the commitment and the conscious decision to do ever better, have strengthened. Again, gratitude and discipline have been the magic bullets. Scott Peck's dedication to the truth has been for me, the most challenging and yes, painful aspect of the discipline lesson. I have had to face my own demons, identify and acknowledge my own maladaptive beliefs and resolve to let go of "precious" although neurotic parts of myself.

In their innocence children can be painfully accurate in their assessment of parental behaviours and motivations. They can quite effectively *put you in your place* at times when it might be inconvenient and/or embarrassing. By way of an example, I recall an instance when, as I was complaining to my 17 year-old son Joshua about not having time to write this book on motherhood, he calmly asked "Shouldn't you wait until we're grown and raised to write about your experience of motherhood?" So I did! LOL. Grudgingly at times, I drag myself down the path to heightened consciousness hoping that if I model the journey, the children's will be less marred by "unnecessary" suffering.

As I wrote these words,
it was my hope that:

Every page would in some way represent a little piece of light

Every page would ease you along the path of adjustment to motherhood

The lessons that you hopefully learn from reading these pages would be generously applied to every potentially stressful aspect of your life

The children would benefit from your journey

The children would benefit from your evolution

Your rise in consciousness would inform their rise

IN CONSCIOUSNESS

EARLY DAYS

In the early days, feelings of being trapped and isolated could predominate. It is never too early to challenge the negative statements and reach out for assistance. See whether you recognize the following in yourself.

Trapped

I feel trapped. Trapped in a web of responsibility.

Shackled by expectations to conform, by pressure to perform. Pressure self-imposed and pressure other/society imposed. Pressure to be **SUPER-MOM**.

I struggle to free my "self", my tired body, my soul. I struggle to maintain balance, to practice self-lessness, to nurture hope. I struggle daily with disappointment, the realization that in the trenches of child-rearing I am alone, only sometimes visited with partner-assistance. You know what I mean. Those small but sometimes lifesaving bits of help from "the partner."

But invariably, at least once daily, I am overwhelmed with the experience of unconditional love both given and received. Love for and from the children. Then I am refueled. At least temporarily.

And so the cycle goes. You continue to dig deep, to find that sometimes elusive source of never-ending MOMENERGY.

But there will come a time when in a quiet moment you will say to yourself "I have a child at home" and feel a calm, contented joy - not panic. You will remember that this is a sacred trust, a responsibility to be lovingly executed. You will know that you are capable, have access to spiritual help if requested, and a member of a huge group of like-minded individuals.

If we are to significantly impact the world's future in a positive manner, the early years must become a priority. The seeds that we plant now will bear fruit later. Any good farmer knows just how much love and attention is required in order to produce a healthy crop. But without knowledge of the requirements necessary for that particular crop's prosperity, the results would be less than optimal. In addition to unconditional love, information about the journey through motherhood provides an advantage.

On the road to conscious spiritual evolution there is no such thing as *wasted* time. Every attempt at improved functioning is important.

NEVER GIVE UP

Do not underestimate your capacity to grow and develop into a conscious, spiritually evolved being.

**KNOW THAT YOU ARE ON
A SPIRITUAL JOURNEY**

**A JOURNEY TO THE RISE
IN CONSCIOUSNESS**

OF BOTH YOURSELF

AS WELL AS YOUR PRECIOUS CHARGES

REMEMBER

YOU ARE NOT ALONE

The stressors are real. Your distress is valid.

Practice optimism. Challenge the negative maladaptive thoughts at every turn.

Accept the responsibility willingly.

Know what you believe.

Try to get clarity in terms of your goals. What do you want most for your children? Honestly assess those goals and decide which ones might need to be altered or adjusted.

Invariably, unconditional love is essential.

Be prepared for discipline and practice. Be prepared to work on yourself.

Talk to others honestly and openly about their experiences with motherhood.

Read what you can on the topic.

Do not wallow in self-pity.

Enjoy the nest full.

Be present. Be grateful.

To the best of your ability, take care of yourself.

Do not be ashamed to admit to your difficulty.

If the struggle becomes overwhelming or unbearable -

SEEK PROFESSIONAL HELP

<u>BECAUSE MY MOTHER LOVED ME</u>

BECAUSE MY MOTHER LOVED ME
I KNOW MY VALUE

BECAUSE GOD LOVES ME
I KNOW MY DIVINITY

BECAUSE THEY BOTH LOVED ME
I KNOW THAT I CAN LOVE

BECAUSE I CAN LOVE
MY CHILDREN CAN LEARN THEIR VALUE

AND SO ON AND SO ON
AND SO ON............

WHY ALL THIS TALK ABOUT MOTHERHOOD?

You might wonder, "Why all this
talk about motherhood?"

Well, the way I see it, there is
always room for more love.

Imagine a world where every child is cherished.

Imagine a world where every child
is taught his/her value.

Imagine a world where every
child is made a priority.

Imagine a world where every
child is shown respect.

Now, imagine a world where these children
grow into wonderful, conscious adults.

Do you see why "all this talk
about motherhood?"

It's not just about this parent or
that child. It's about all of us,

COLLECTIVELY.

With a critical mass of loving, evolved individuals, we could all live in light and love.

WE COULD EXPERIENCE A GLOBAL RISE IN CONSCIOUSNESS

REFERENCES

Peck, Morgan Scott (1978). <u>The Road Less Traveled</u>. New York: Simon & Schuster.

Weiten, W. & Lloyd, M. (2000). Psychology Applied to Modern Life. Wadsworth/Thompson Learning.

White Eagle (1978). <u>The Quiet Mind</u>. The White Eagle Publishing Trust. New Lands. LISS. Hampshire. UK.

Zukav, Gary (1989). <u>The Seat of the Soul</u>. New York: Simon & Schuster.

Printed in the United States
By Bookmasters